FOOTBALL AND THE DECLINE OF BRITAIN

Football and the Decline of Britain

James Walvin
Reader in History, University of York

MACMILLAN

First published 1986

Published by
THE MACMILLAN PRESS LTD
Houndmills, Basingstoke, Hampshire RG21 2XS
and London
Companies and representatives
throughout the world

Typeset by Wessex Typesetters
(Division of The Eastern Press Ltd)
Frome, Somerset.

Printed in Great Britain by
Anchor Brendon Ltd.
Tiptree, Essex

British Library Cataloguing in Publication Data
Walvin, James
Football and the decline of Britain.
1. Soccer—Social aspects—Great Britain
—History
I. Title
306'.483   GV944.G7
ISBN 0–333–42276–7 (hardcover)
ISBN 0–333–42277–5 (paperback)

Contents

Preface

More than ten years ago I wrote a history of soccer and imagined that I would never return to the topic. Instead I moved on to other (sometimes related) issues in modern social history. But in the intervening years I tried to keep abreast of the academic and popular literature about the game; a literature which continued to issue profusely from the presses. My personal attachment to the game was much less persistent though I still thought of myself as a football fan, committed especially to the fortunes of one particular team. There was, it is true, a host of family and social reasons which conspired to keep me away from the game which had, for all the years I could remember, proved utterly irresistible. But the loss of youthful enthusiasm was not the only major factor responsible. Increasingly there were trends in the modern game which I thoroughly disliked and which served to repel me – and countless others. Recited in cold print, many of these factors seem merely the quaint excuses of an ageing male unhappy with the behaviour of younger people. None the less, there were objective social trends which alienated me: violence – on and off the field, the organised chanting of obscenities, the apparently baffling rise of racial abuse – all of these, in addition to the often bizarre behaviour of players and managers, and the gleeful and sometimes sordid coverage given to their more idiosyncratic utterances and actions, created a sense that the game had changed – for the worse. And yet football itself remained an endlessly fascinating game; at its best, quite the most exhilarating contest of skills and strength. Indeed, it is these basic attractions which have enabled football to become so universally popular, watched and played by millions around the world. It is one of the most successful and abiding of all British exports; shaped and fashioned in Britain and successfully transplanted to most societies around the world.

In its homeland, the game in recent years has plunged deeper and deeper into a crisis, partly of its own making, partly thrust upon it by external forces over which football has little or no control. It is in order to address what I take to be the sources of the game's crisis that I have written this book. But the book would have not been written without the catastrophic events of the early summer of 1985 when, at two unrelated games, ninety-four innocent people lost their lives.

There followed a natural and quite extraordinary outpouring of explanations for those two terrible incidents. The more I read, the more confused I became, for there seemed little common ground between a host of competing explanations (save for the fact that most sought to locate the causes in broader ailments afflicting British life). This book therefore developed as an attempt to offer my own interpretation, and it tries to look beyond the immediate roots of those two events – the fire in Bradford and the riot in Brussels – attempting instead to locate them in a much broader historically shaped context. I cannot pretend that what follows is uniquely a work of history, for although I am by training and profession a historian and although this work is, I hope, clearly influenced by that fact, I have tried to write a book which is as much personal statement as it is cold historical assessment.

It was written in the summer of 1985, in the immediate aftermath of those two disasters but, as will become clear, it was rooted in earlier research into the history of the game and a familiarity with the subsequent research and writing on football. While the argument is my own, the development of my views has been influenced by some excellent scholarly studies of football published in recent years. But although concerned specifically with football the pages that follow try to locate the game – its rise and problems – within the context of the major changes in recent British history. It is in a sense an attempt to study what has happened to Britain, but more especially England, through the fluctuations in the game of football. Thus it is only in part a study of football; it is as much an essay on social change in England over the past twenty-five years.

The book is concerned with a specifically English experience but it would be wrong to suggest that much of what is said is uniquely English. Although the disasters were English, and the subsequent punishments were properly directed at English football, many of the games' difficulties are to be found in Scotland. It is true that Scottish authorities acted sooner than the English against some of the problems afflicting their game (notably drunkenness), but that was only because their problems were worse. Much of what follows can be equally applied to Scotland; but the book is concerned primarily with England.

JAMES WALVIN

Acknowledgements

The initial encouragement to write this book came from Liz Knights; without her prompting I would not have begun the task. Thereafter I was greatly helped by a number of colleagues and friends. Avner Offer, as usual, provided a string of ideas and suggestions. David Goodhart influenced me through a number of lengthy conversations. Two friends, both sociologists, read the completed manuscript and their detailed criticism helped me to improve the final version and I am happy to record my thanks to Bob Coles and Steve Fenton. Similarly I was fortunate to have the comments of Bill Murray – a fund of knowledge about Scottish football. The book was written partly in York and partly in Australia, where I benefited from the healthy scepticism of the social history group at Adelaide, as well as the facilities at my disposal in the libraries and history departments at La Trobe University, and the Universities of Adelaide and Queensland. Pamela Doweswell managed to transcribe my scrawl, promptly and efficiently, into readable typescript. My elder son, Gavin, helped me with some of the initial research and regularly criticised my ideas – and much else besides.

JAMES WALVIN

1 Prologue: Whatever Happened to the People's Game?

For more than a century the game of soccer has been widely recognised as the British national game. Notwithstanding the claims of cricket to represent the English at play in the summer, it was soccer which evolved, from ancient folk customs, to become the most popular game in the highly urbanised and industrialised world of the late nineteenth century. Highly disciplined in conduct and regulation, enormously popular among legions of men and boys from all social classes, commercially attractive to investors and ancillary backers, football by the mid-1880s was thriving as no other game had done before. Watched by tens of thousands, in new purpose-built stadiums, played by thousands more – thanks in large measure to the game's unique qualities of cheapness, simple organisation and the ease of organising football for new generations of compulsorarily educated school boys – soccer was universally accepted as 'the people's game'. It is true, however, that this catchy epithet ignored the crucial fact that, by and large, only the male half of the population loved the game. None the less, few could deny the unique position – acquired in a very brief period – which soccer had come to occupy among that generation of men born into late Victorian and early Edwardian society. By 1895, the great Victorian all-round sportsman, C. B. Fry, felt constrained to declare:

> The great and widespread interest in football is a manifest fact. So much so that nowadays it is frequently urged that cricket can no longer be regarded as our 'national game', in the true sense of the word. Football, it is claimed, has now the first place in the popular heart.[1]

Few could doubt that football had, in the words of one Liverpool gentleman, become 'the game of the busy classes and consequently of the people'.[2]

By the turn of the century, football had also become one of Britain's most successful exports. The game had been transplanted

1

around the globe by Britons travelling, working or settling abroad. Widely played throughout western Europe, the game had also taken root in more 'exotic' regions. In a world which welcomed British goods, services and skills, football proved equally attractive. It appealed to boys and youths with plenty of free time and abundant energies, to organised working men with a certain amount of leisure time and spare cash for recreation – and to those educational groups which encouraged physical activity as part of a rounded education (a belief assiduously promoted, at home and abroad, by proponents of the English public school ideals). It is true that football was not completely successful in exporting itself around the world and there were to remain regions and countries which defied the advance of the game (most notably in North America and the white dominions). In an era of massive expansion of their global, political and material power, the British transplanted their language, institutions, religions and economic interests throughout the world. It was perfectly natural that their games and recreations should go with them. Indeed, long after other British influence disappeared or dwindled to insignificance (as British economic power receded before the advancing influence of other nations), football survived, in some cases to become the sole reminder of an era of British pre-eminence.

It was, however, in Britain – and especially in the industrial towns of the North and the Midlands – that football found its strongest support. In 1892, the periodical, *Nineteenth Century*, published an article entitled 'The New Football Mania' which sought to describe the footballing phenomenon:

> In all our large towns, and most of the small ones, north of Birmingham to the Tweed, from September to April, Saturday is consecrated to football. Saturday evenings are devoted to football symposia, and the newspapers issue special editions.

Local teams were 'better known than the local members of Parliament' and support had spread across the divides of age and sex: 'Many old people and women are so caught by it that they would not, on any ordinary account, miss a local match.' The resulting crowds were – (at least in the eyes of their betters) dirty and sometimes offensive:

> The multitude flock to the field in their workaday dirt, and with their workaday adjectives very loose on their tongues. In

Lancashire and the Black Country it is really surprising what a number of emphatic and even mysterious expletives may be heard on these Saturday afternoons. Some of them are, however, remarkably unpleasant and not fit for a lady's ears, even to the remotest echo!

'It is,' the article continued, 'ludicrous to see how boys of a very tender age get possessed of a frenzy at some of these matches.'[3]

At the grounds, and travelling to and from the games on trams and excursion trains, these football fans were, by the mid-1890s, already famous for their boisterous high spirits, their noise and general vulgarity. One proponent of railway nationalisation, in 1893, would have more support, claimed a critic, if he could 'retain a separate carriage or a separate train – if not a separate line of railway – for vociferous football teams on their return journey'.[4] Yet the excitement and exuberance of the football fans was not restricted to any one social class, though clearly the biggest single element in the crowds were working-class males. The modern game of football had, after all, emerged from the public schools; had been codified, propagated and encouraged by the public schools and their ex-pupils. Not surprisingly then, men of a higher social station could also be seen enjoying the game – as players and spectators. Commenting on football in London in 1901, one writer noted.

Whilst there are ragged urchins kicking paper balls in back alleys in Fulham and Whitechapel, there are top-hatted, frock-coated gentlemen with grey beards, who sorrow over the passing of sixty winters, but who yet on this same afternoon are kicking the boards in front of them on the stand at Queen's Club, so high and so uncontrollable is their excitement as they watch the fortunes of a great match.[5]

The support shown for football in the late years of the century was increasingly denounced by men of a certain disposition; men who disliked fanaticism and unbridled enthusiasm among the common people; who disliked the ascendant commercialism of contemporary football and who saw in the mass excitement of the football crowd a collective plebeian passion which seemed an unhealthy social force. In 1899, for instance (shortly after the Cup Final) *The Ethical World* denounced the prevailing trends in football:

No sober-minded person acquainted with the life of the Midland and Northern towns can fail to perceive that football has passed from a wholesome and enjoyable game into an all-absorbing mania of the million, devouring and displacing every other interest and occupation, and developing all the worst forms of professionalism and betting . . . We do not grudge 70,000 spectators their enjoyment of a game, but we also protest against the deliberate encouragement of a form of competition which becomes every year less and less recreative and more and more 'commercial', by the leaders of our great parties.

Under commercial pressure, it was argued, football 'degenerates more and more into organised brutality and breeds brutality in the spectators'.[6] This critique was vigorously denied later by a correspondent who felt that the allegation of brutality 'has no adequate foundation'.[7] None the less, for our purposes it is instructive that there *were* late century critics who saw in the game a series of unacceptable social trends; of popular and collective zeal which spilled over into turbulence of sporting professionalism (hence a denial of the public school amateur sporting ethic), of sporting commercialism – none more disliked than the widespread plebeian passion for gambling.

It is important not to divorce this analysis of football from the broader development of popular recreations and leisure – of which soccer was only the most striking (because so massively popular and therefore inescapable). These same years witnessed the emergence of a variety of recreational pursuits and sports which, though familiar to the modern reader, were relatively new developments in the social life of the British people. Organised holidays, notably the mass exodus from urban areas on the Bank Holidays (introduced in 1871), the epic and (to foreigners at least) the perplexing rush to the seaside resorts in the summer season, these and a host of new or reformed games and leisure pursuits collectively transformed the social lives of the British people. This was especially striking among working people, growing numbers of whom were able to enjoy many of the newer material benefits disgorged by the mature British economy by virtue of their increased (though none the less limited) purchasing power. Moreover, there were wide sections of working-class life, notably those men in the heavier basic industries, whose working conditions were protected by powerful trade unions, and who found themselves with free time – leisure time – in which to enjoy their favourite recreations or sports. Football, like the seaside trip, the committal to choral and brass band music-making, the growing cult of gardening and allotments, or the mass proliferation of music halls throughout urban Britain – all these and more were, in essence, functions of fundamental changes in the economic life of the nation. Although each element in the complicated history of the development of modern leisure provides an interesting and colourful story in itself, what is perhaps most revealing is the way the history of leisure offers a telling insight into the fundamental economic and social changes which came to transform the face of urban Britain.

The journal, *The Ethical World*, was highly critical of football and its supporters, but was, nevertheless, a major advocate of working-class leisure – but in a healthier and more wholesome environment than the urban areas which spawned the dominant working-class pleasures:

> The more sensible members of the working-class drift away from the city on one or other of the innumerable day-excursions – to Brighton or Southend, or to homes and friends in provincial towns.

Many, it was claimed, flocked to the local parks and open spaces in their holiday breaks, but 'Of the great residue that hovers all day about the music-halls and public houses of the city let us be silent, conscience-stricken'.[8]

What concerned large numbers of late century social critics was that football had lost its way and merely become a reflection of a host of unattractive characteristics of urban life. Where the game had once been promoted as a healthy and disciplined recreation for working men whose lives were, by and large, blighted by the miseries of city life, it had, by 1900, become a highly commercialised weekly ritual, which encouraged passionate, local (often religious) fanaticism, collective and vulgar rowdiness and a general plebeian assertiveness which seemed (to outsiders at least) undesirably divisive in an already divided nation. For good or ill, football had sunk its roots deep into urban, especially working-class, life long before the end of Victoria's reign. Furthermore, for all the criticism which was directed (often unfairly) at football in those years, the game's defenders and proponents were no less vociferous and assertive. Of course, what gave the game its unique hold over so many people was its fundamental appeal to players and spectators alike. Easy and enjoyable to play – and encouraged from early years in the new Board schools – enjoyable to watch, accessible to even the meanest of urban communities, rooted in local institutions (churches, Sunday schools, factories and trade unions), football was – with certain regional exceptions – the undisputed game of working-class life. In the words of one commentator in 1895: 'The nation, we are told, is a democracy, and the game of the people must be accepted as the game of the nation.'[9] Though the game's critics were many and aggressive, there could be no denying its following. 'No words of ours,' wrote one man in 1886, 'can adequately describe the present popularity of football with the public – a popularity which, though great in metropolis, is infinitely greater in the large provincial towns.'[10] This is a far cry from the situation facing the national game a century later.

The end of the season, in the early summer of 1985, saw the lowest ebb in the fortunes of British football. Two major footballing disasters, at Bradford and Brussels, cost ninety-four lives and many more injuries, not only gave the game's shortcomings an unprecedented international scrutiny but stimulated a public and political outcry and a consequent hasty series of punitive measures against the English game. First, a horrific fire, in an ancient and generally unsuitable stadium at Bradford killed fifty-six and horribly burned many others, at what was to be an enjoyable and celebratory, end-of-season, third division game. The home team had gained promotion to the second division and the crowd was consequently bigger – and television cameras were there to record the occasion. Instead they filmed a disaster which swept over spectators in a matter of minutes. There followed, inevitably perhaps, an extraordinary outpouring of grief – and recrimination – with the government ordering a judicial enquiry (to study also a serious disturbance at Birmingham on the same day). But few people who read the press or watched the television analysis were left in any doubt that the basic roots of the tragedy were to be found in the antiquated physical structures and outlook of the game itself. A palpably outdated stand, in a club which lacked the financial wherewithal or support to modernise had proved a death trap. More fundamentally, it offered a ghastly illustration of a problem which was commonplace throughout the ninety-two professional league clubs. Many, if not most, of them were old institutions; relics of the hey-day of soccer when the local team provided one of the few leisure outlets for working people. Since the Second World War, however, the clubs' appeal has greatly diminished and as their supporters thinned, often to skeletal proportions, the vital income similarly evaporated. What survived was the physical plant; the stadiums whose facilities went unchallenged two generations ago but which now stand revealed not merely as unpleasant and uncomfortable but, under certain circumstances, positively dangerous.

Within weeks of the Bradford disaster, another major incident at a football ground, the 55-year-old Heysel stadium in Brussels, cost thirty-eight lives and scores of injuries. Friction between opposing Liverpool and Juventus fans at the European Cup Final led to attacks by sections of the Liverpool contingent against their neighbouring rivals. In the resulting confusion and rush to escape those attacks, panic, crush and collapsing walls claimed the lives of thirty-eight fans, all but a handful Italians, and caused many more injuries. The unbearable scenes of suffering and carnage were transmitted to a worldwide audience in more than eighty countries. The consequent outcry was extraordinary. In a confusion of denunciation and recrimination, the overwhelming majority of critics – led by those in the stadium when the accident occurred – blamed the Liverpool fans for the tragedy. It was also the deadly culmination of years of aggression and damage visited by English fans upon stadiums and cities throughout western Europe, from Helsinki to Barcelona. It was immediately clear that Liverpool Football Club and English (and perhaps even British) football would be made to pay for the sins of a relatively small band of marauding fans. Within days, all English clubs – of all sorts and conditions – had been banned from Europe: later FIFA ordered all English clubs not to play outside England itself. The country which had developed and then exported the game found itself ostracised and reviled in the world's footballing fraternity.

There seemed few people lacking an explanation for the Brussels disaster. Indeed, in the proliferation of published views in the aftermath of Brussels, critics of different and even conflicting persuasions were united in one point; that the Brussels disaster was proof of their own particular worldview and analysis. From the sections on the left, Brussels was – in some indefinable way – an example of the heartlessness and commercial crudeness of capitalism (in this case in the form of the commercial interests behind football).[11] Another view on the left was to impute the 'macho' violence of young football fans to that jingoism so successfully whipped up three years earlier in the Falklands campaign. ('Mrs Thatcher rejoiced and the *Sun* crowed "Gotcha!" to war in the Falklands, but both spoke of national shame when "our boys" went to kill in Brussels').[12] The Prime Minister herself offered her own explanations (a vague account of the demoralising affect of general prosperity, plus the influence of violence in Ulster and during the recent miners' strike). More romantic souls saw an explanation in the decline of a traditional working-class 'community spirit'; Mrs Whitehouse viewed it as further proof of England's moral decay.

The popular newspapers ran their most lurid banner-headlines and their blow-up photos of heaps of corpses enabled them to reduce still further their few words of printed text. Cartoonists vied with the headline writers to denounce the Liverpudlian perpetrators of the disaster: rats on the one hand (*The Observer*), fascist punks on the other (*Sunday Express*).[13] Explanations were as numerous as they were conflicting and unconvincing; solutions (though the 'problem' was not always identified) no less varied. It was impossible to pick a clear path through the remarkable confusion which reigned in the press in the aftermath of Brussels. Indeed, it is this very confusion – of analysis and cure – which stands out as perhaps *the* most striking feature of the response to Brussels. And as if to compound this confusion, the judge enquiring into the Bradford fire was ordered to add Brussels to his agenda; the links between the two were hard to see.

In all this welter of print, few expressed any doubts that football was in a deep – perhaps even a terminal – crisis. One of Britain's best sporting journalists wrote, 'One more corpse was carried from the Brussels stadium last night. Soccer itself – draped in the Union Jack. It deserved to be spat upon.'[14] It is perfectly natural that people should feel revulsion at such wanton death and destruction. But how, we need to enquire, could football have come to such a pass; how could a game of such unparalleled popularity and global importance come to be associated with (and perhaps even the cause of) such scenes of violence and death? Indeed, the question arises; what precisely *is* the relationship between what we saw at Brussels (or Bradford) and the game of football? It seems unlikely that any satisfactory or complete explanation will be found solely by scrutinising the game itself; in the recent past, just as in its long-term history, football has been more a reflector than a creator of social trends. If it is true that the game has, in the 1980s as in the 1880s, often been shaped and directed by social forces not of its own making, it is important that we seek to locate these recent events not merely in their immediate and perhaps contingent context, but also in their broader setting. It is perfectly clear that the disasters at Bradford and Brussels were, at one level, mere accidents; they were not bound, *inevitably*, to happen. Yet it is also true that the forces which conspired to make both of those disasters possible were, at once, more confusing and long term than we might imagine by merely examining the internal proceedings of the game itself. What follows is then an attempt to fit the events of Bradford and Brussels in a historical and social setting which makes both more easily understood.

The events of the summer of 1985 will doubtless prove a turning point in the history of the national game, more especially if the proposed palliatives are enforced (stricter crowd control, fire control, membership cards and a closer scrutiny of old stadiums). Yet it is also true that football has, like its parent society, been experiencing a major transformation over the past generation. By the mid-1980s, football was still by far the most popular of all spectator sports, well in advance of its nearest rival, rugby. The annual evidence, published through the government's statistical office, is clear enough. In its report on national statistics for 1983, this was, for our purposes, the key point: 'Football is by far the most popular sport watched by men – an average of 6% of all men, and 8% of those in both the 16 to 19 and 20 to 34 age groups, watched football in 1983.'

Rugby, the second most popular spectator sport was watched by only 2 per cent.[15] In common with most spectator sports, the kind of people watching football tended to be younger – and male. Other social surveys in the late 1970s and early 1980s provide more detailed substance to this general pattern, though in essence their findings will surprise no one who attends the game or merely watches it (and its crowds) on television. In 1980 it was described as follows: 'a football crowd emerges as predominantly male, younger rather than elderly, and socially mixed though with an over-representation of skilled manual workers.'[16] What is crucial, however – and here the statistical data may provide certain clues to the changing nature (and problems) of football – is the age structure of the typical football crowd. Supporters aged 20 and under form more than 20 per cent of football crowds, and although attendances have fallen fairly regularly since the Second World War, this younger section of the crowd has increased. Thus, the young have come to exert a proportionately greater presence, and possibly impact, in the make-up of the typical football crowd. Furthermore, this pattern has also been detected among the fans who travel away to watch football. Older fans, increasingly, tend not to travel, with the result that the typical travelling fan is a younger man.[17] In a sense this is merely an accentuation of an older pattern; those with the necessary free time, spare cash and freedom from family commitments to enable them to travel across the country had traditionally been young. More recently, however, the troubles at football grounds have repelled ever more older men who would otherwise have watched the game, persuading them not to attend. It seems clear that the make-up of the typical football crowd has changed quite crucially.

More striking still is the general decline in football attendance. In the 1984/5 season, fewer than 18 million people watched league games; this is well below half the numbers who turned out to watch football in its post-war boom years. It is easy to understand why the game seemed so attractive in the late 1940s, as the nation tried to shrug off its wartime restraints and drabness and to return to the pleasures and pursuits familiar in more peaceful times. Nor was football alone in enjoying a boom. Seaside resorts were, quite literally, invaded by unprecedented millions of holiday-makers in the summer months. The railway carried record numbers to Blackpool; in 1949 half a million travelled to Scarborough by motor coach. In that same year 32 million people took their holidays at the seaside, a growing proportion of them travelling by road. The cinema too enjoyed good years, with 1635 million attendances in 1946. More than three-quarters of the total population visited the cinema at some time or other, with attendance being more regular and frequent lower down the social scale. Like the cinema, football enjoyed its golden years in the late 1940s; massive queues were the norm and the only restraint on attendance was the physical capacity of the grounds themselves. Even the amateur game could attract tens of thousands: the Amateur Cup Final was switched to Wembley in 1949 – and promptly attracted 90,000 people.[18] That year saw the peak of football's fortunes – with more than 41 million spectators.

Clearly the pattern of the post-war years could not maintain itself. As the austerity of the 1940s began, grudgingly and gradually, to give way to the encroaching material prosperity of the early 1950s, the leisure patterns of the British began to change. Between 1952–4 football attendance declined by 6 million; by 1955–6 it stood at 33.3 million. Five years later it had slid further to 28.6 million. The English World Cup victory of 1966 restored attendances a little, pushing them just above 30 million.[19] By 1980 it was down to 23 million; four years later below 18 million. The attendance in 1983–4 was 36 per cent lower than in 1971–2.

Which ever way we break down these general figures, the results make bleak reading for the clubs themselves. In the First Division, the average gate has shrunk, to 18 856 in 1983–4; in 1971–2 it stood at 31 829. In Division Four, the average game of 2822 in 1983–4 compares to 4981 in 1971–2. There are inevitably, of course, some marked exceptions to these general patterns. Manchester United, for example, in 1983–4 had a home attendance which was almost 2½ times the league average.[20] Moreover, although this overall decline is to be seen throughout the league, the most serious decline is in the lower divisions. Indeed, the total average for Divisions 2, 3 and 4 is only a little higher than that for Division 1.

Long before the rumblings from bigger, wealthier clubs in the autumn of 1985, the evidence existed of the need to reform the league structure. Moreover, that reform had long been recommended by serious and informed critics of the game, notably in the Chester Report of 1968. Whatever the precise outcome – 'Super-League', a move back to regional leagues, smaller leagues or part-time clubs – it seems clear that the league structure and the uneven attendances will lead to major reorganisation of the game. This process seems likely to be greatly assisted by the initial failure to conclude agreements with the TV companies in 1985 and the consequent decline in income for the clubs.

It is in the lower reaches of these divisions that the material and financial problems of the modern game are to be found in abundance. Add to this crucial difficulty the seminal fact that large numbers of the smaller, older clubs are located in areas of the country now blighted by industrial decay and general economic decline, and it can readily be seen that many football clubs have come to mirror the broader economic difficulties facing their towns and regions. While it may be true that in the inter-war years the game was a cheap entertainment and escape for those communities afflicted by the depression; the present-day game is no longer cheap. In fact its admission prices are not out of line with other spectator sports and commercial entertainments, but the cost of admission is cited, in recent surveys of the game, as a major reason for not attending. Furthermore, even among those who *do* watch the game two out of three fans felt that they were charged too much for admission.[21] Again, it is worth repeating that this decline is shared by other forms of entertainment. Nevertheless, the decline in football attendance has not been as dramatic or far-reaching as the fall in cinema going[22] – though both owe their spiralling fortunes to very similar social origins; basically the popular shift in general leisure interests and an overall transformation in popular cultural habits among the British people.

It is obvious that many of the factors which have served to deprive football (and other recreations) of its followers are external to the game itself. There is little that football clubs or their controlling organisations can do to alter the social forces – notably changes in leisure patterns – which have conspired against them for a generation or more. Equally, there are crucial areas where the game could (but has, by and large, failed to) enhance its own attractiveness, notably by improving the physical facilities of the football stadiums. It needs to be stressed that even the most comfortable and modernised of stadiums will fail to win back supporters unless the local team can prove attractive to watch. (Some of the most modern facilities (Coventry, for instance) fail to attract more than modest crowds.) And it is at this point, once more, that the problem comes full circle for if the quality of football on offer falls below expectations, potential spectators will simply take their custom and their money to other forms of diversion. It is, of course, undeniable that there is now a myriad of entertainments and diversion bidding for the time and the money of the consumer. Television is an obvious – and remarkably cheap and convenient – alternative. So too are the varied activities in and around the household; DIY, gardening, car maintenance and the like, all of which have blossomed since the 1950s with the massive and quite unpredictable growth in home and car ownership.[23] This image may, in many respects, seem out of kilter in a society which since the mid-1970s has been disfigured by economic recession and massive unemployment. None the less, the hardship of substantial minorities cannot deflect the main thrust of the case; that the greater material benefits for many, the more varied material offerings of a rapidly transforming economy, have served to expand the leisure prospects and the aspirations of many millions of people. There are, quite simply, many more (and for some people, more attractive) spare time alternatives to the local football ground. And the stark evidence is to be seen in the yards of empty terracing and seating available at most professional games.

There are, however, important qualifications to be made to this dismal image of the contemporary game. First, the game is watched – on television – by many millions of people who do not attend the games. BBC's *Match of the Day* has attracted an audience of 10 million. Whether such audiences can survive both the excessive exposure of football and the likely repulsion from the game following the television coverage of the recent disasters, remains to be seen. Indeed, the 1985 season began with no TV coverage of English football, as both sides were locked into dispute which embraced much more than mere finance. At the heart of the matter lay a host of disagreements notably among the clubs, about the desirability of televising football; about whether football on TV might in fact be aiding the decline in paying spectators. It is perfectly true that television has enabled unprecedented numbers of people to watch the game; certainly many more than could be accommodated in the stadiums themselves. But, as we shall see, television has proved a mixed blessing for the game of football. Indeed, much of the widespread outrage so commonly expressed about the game in the summer of 1985 stems directly from the television coverage of the disasters at Bradford and Brussels.

Another qualification is again both obvious and yet normally ignored. While the professional game flounders, football continues to be unprecedentedly popular as a participatory sport. There are more teams, at all amateur levels, competing for 'public' sporting space that can be adequately catered for. Something like 1½ million men and boys play football each weekend. For many years past the amateur, *ad hoc* and popular game has thrived as its professional counterpart declined. Once more, this is part of a much broader pattern. Sporting activity and participation has, over the past thirty years or so, shown a quite remarkable increase, while spectator sports have shown a comparable decline.[24] Clearly any analysis – of why more males play football while fewer watch it – will be incomplete and unconvincing if it seeks an explanation uniquely from the game itself. Here – and at a myriad other points – the explanations of football's changing patterns (and problems) must be located within a broader social context.

After a fashion, this is what many of the post-Brussels critics have sought to do; to proffer analyses of one particular difficulty facing football (violence) by reference to the contemporary ills of modern Britain. Unfortunately, few of these explanations have been convincing (to this author at least), if only because most have been rooted in preconceived analyses which were merely 'proved' by the events in Brussels. With some notable and honourable exceptions, much of that commentary was written in ignorance (admittedly in haste) of much of the evidence readily available. Few were so dismissive of this important body of research than the Prime Minister herself, who merely brushed it aside as mere ephemera, of no real use in the search for practical solutions.

To compound the generally shallow nature of recent analyses of contemporary ills – of which the post-Brussels debate is a classic example – is the fact that few observers, if any, are informed by a sense of history. Not the history available only to a professional scholar, but that sense of the immediate, short-term past, an understanding of which is crucial if our grasp of these (or related) matters is not to be partial, incomplete and therefore inadequate. C. B. Fry's comment, of ninety years ago, is equally true today: 'The great and widespread interest in football is a manifest fact.' The reasons for that interest are, however, utterly different. At the turn of the century, *The Times* (and many others) thought that football, and other games, formed an ideal antidote to the problems of urban and industrial life:

> It is, indeed, in athletic games, and in the increased hold which they have obtained upon all classes of the community, but especially upon the industrial classes, that the best remedy is to be found for conditions which tend to crowd workers into cities, and to deprive them of some of the requirements of sound physical development.[25]

In June 1985, that same paper argued that football would soon be played 'in fortified amphitheatres with iron cages where there used to be terraces and a breathalyser machine at every turnstile'. Clearly, something quite dramatic has happened to people's perceptions of the national game. Given the changing face of modern Britain, this might not be so surprising.

Part One
People on the Inside

2 Victorian Values: Clubs and Managers

It was evident that the modern English game was in a deep crisis long before the disasters of Bradford and Brussels. Indeed, those terrible events brought to a head a series of problems, endemic to the game, which had long been in need of attention but which had been studiously ignored by clubs and football's governing authorities. The major problem was (and is) the clubs themselves. By and large, they are Victorian and Edwardian institutions, often fiercely resistant to change, determined to maintain their methods and traditions – most of which were forged in an earlier and quite different epoch. Clubs have been 'old fashioned' in the worst of senses; reluctant to change their outlook and their mode of operations. But the clubs were also desperate to benefit from whatever lucrative deal could be clinched with new commercial interests. The end result has been a peculiar amalgam, of old and new; of clubs whose physical appearance has, in many cases, changed little since the early years of the century but who adopt a host of modern money-making tactics and often flamboyant methods of fund-raising.

It is easy to be critical of football clubs, but their difficulties are monumental – though many are undoubtedly self-induced. Moreover, these difficulties are likely to increase substantially in the aftermath of Brussels and Bradford. First and foremost, football clubs are in a serious financial situation. In part that stems from the dramatic decline in the numbers of paying spectators. But this has been compounded by the escalation of costs, most spectacularly by players' wages, which consistently outstrip income. The evidence is clear enough. From their most recently returned financial statements it is possible, in the summer of 1985, to see in stark detail the nature and extent of the problem.

Of the league's ninety-two clubs, precisely half, forty-six, were trading with liabilities in excess of assets. Many, if not most of those clubs are in debt, often to a substantial degree, with all the consequent strain of heavy interest payments. But the most consistent burden is that of wage bills. In the first division, the average is £1.02 million annually. The average in the lower divisions

17

Table 1.1a   Clubs with liabilities exceeding assets

	Accts	Net assets
Chelsea	1984	−£405,642
Watford	1984	−£698,121
Luton Town	1982	−£185,175
West Ham	1984	−£250,703
Birmingham City	1984	−£330,779
Portsmouth	1984	−£373,515
Brighton & Hove Albion	1983	−£645,615
Leeds Utd	1983	−£73,062
Fulham	1984	−£1.386m
Wimbledon	1983	−£211,932
Huddersfield Town	1984	−£88,664
Oldham Athletic	1984	−£135,177
Charlton Athletic	1982	−£391,719
Notts County	1984	−£339,831
Millwall	1982	−£1.32m
Hull City	1983	−£11,174
Bristol City	1981	−£93,903
Bristol Rovers	1983	−£80,626
Derby County	1984	−£630,463
Bournemouth	1983	−£114,519
Brentford	1983	−£215,588
Doncaster Rovers	1983	−£104,199
Plymouth Albion	1983	−£208,802
Wigan Athletic	1983	−£213,176
Bolton Wanderers	1983	−£283,509
Newport County	1983	−£293,321
Lincoln City	1983	−£100,229
Swansea City	1983	−£837,591
Orient	1983	−£147,701
Preston North End	1983	−£100,187
Cambridge Utd	1983	−£11,920
Bury	1984	−£96,142
Tranmere Rovers	1983	−£58,418
Swindon Town	1984	−£148,659
Colchester Utd	1984	−£93,849
Crewe Alexandra	1983	−£23,754
Port Vale	1983	−£107,069
Mansfield Town	1984	−£402,174
Wrexham	1983	−£114,363
Exeter City	1984	−£265,600
Hartlepool Utd	1979	−£79,045
Southend Utd	1981	−£133,652
Halifax Town	1983	−£177,882
Stockport County	1981	−£287,451
Northampton Town	1982	−£87,810
Torquay Utd	1983	−£192,095

Table 1.1b   Club wages

		The big spenders –	
		rankings by wages bills	
	Division	Turnover	Wages
Arsenal	1	£2.6m	£1.8m
Manchester United	1	£6m	£1.76m
Liverpool	1	£3.95m	£1.67m
Tottenham Hotspur	1	£4.76m	£1.66m
Everton	1	£3.28m	£1.2m
West Ham	1	£2.25m	£1.13m
Aston Villa	1	£2.38m	£1.07m
Brighton & Hove Albion	2	£2.27m	£1.2m
Ipswich Town	1	£2.56m	£1m
Newcastle United	1	£2.87m	£0.94m
West Bromwich Albion	1	£1.59m	£0.88m
Birmingham City	2	£0.97m	£0.87m

Source: The Times, 22 July 1985.

is correspondingly smaller – but so too are those clubs' takings. The annual average wage bill is £0.43m (2nd), £0.39m (3rd) and £0.24m (4th). Football was, until the past generation, characterised by a parsimony towards its players which derived substantially from a number of early twentieth-century social and economic attitudes. The early game bitterly resisted the encroachment of professional, waged players, preferring instead to maintain the pioneering amateur traditions which had informed the public school game. When the modern professional game established itself it did so through wages which were strictly limited, not simply by being an adjunct to contemporary plebeian earnings, but by rigid regulation and ceilings maintained by the clubs and their supervisory organisations. Not until the 1960s did English football break with this mould, and only then by concerted union organisation and legal action.[1] Thereafter the situation was instantly and dramatically changed. There followed a major escalation of wages, not merely of the best players, but throughout the leagues. And while it remains true that the wages for *most* footballers remain moderate, there was a contagion of high settlements, with bonuses, lump sum 'loyalty' payments and a host of costly expenses (negotiated increasingly by players' agents). As players' freedom of movement was guaranteed by the law, and as foreign clubs sought to secure the services of British players, there was a permanent inflationary dimension to pay agreements between clubs and players. Although it is true that even the biggest English clubs cannot compete with the wages offered by a number of European clubs (in Germany, Italy and Spain especially), by English levels of earnings the prominent footballers were able, by 1985, to earn extraordinary wages. In 1984, Arsenal paid one man upwards of £80 000.[2] And all this was in addition to the accumulating interest payments, primarily on transfer fees (most of which are paid on credit) agreed some time earlier but now difficult or onerous to complete. The previously inflated transfer fees had collapsed by the mid-1980s; leaving clubs with heavy payments but unable to recoup by selling players at high prices. It was as if English football clubs were in a financial tail-spin from which it seemed impossible to pull out.

The clubs themselves are obviously acutely aware of their own and their colleagues' difficulties. Indeed, in October 1982, they commissioned an enquiry into the viability of the game's structure and its finances.

Characteristically, most of the resulting recommendations were rejected.[3] It is perfectly true that the clubs are not entirely their own masters but are bound, to a quite extraordinary degree, by the governing bodies of the FA and the Football League which interject a number of restrictions and controls on the way clubs can manage themselves. In the aftermath of the disasters, football's financial well-being is being removed even further from the clubs' own control by the penal intervention of UEFA, FIFA and – most punitive of all – by the British government itself. The changes in the law relating to football grounds, recommended by the Popplewell enquiry,[4] will unquestionably place severe financial strains on clubs already staggering beneath a burden of accumulated debt, declining income and the attention of hostile critics.

It is also true that the clubs have, traditionally, appeared incapable of keeping their own house in good financial order. The obvious but impressionistic evidence available to all spectators is merely the casual proof of a point easily documented by research. Clubs which lavish small fortunes on buying a player of modest abilities, which keep their players in a style to which they were unaccustomed (and which perhaps they do not even deserve) have none the less failed to invest comparable sums in physical amenities for their fans. It seems at best perverse, at worst wrong-headed, to award players (and managers) salaries in excess of all but the most senior business executives and yet to claim, as the clubs do frequently and collectively, that there is no money for ground improvement and safety measures. Understandably, this apparent contradiction in financial policy – or rather the directing of resources towards selected areas of the game – has failed to impress both the reading public and those politicians who have been drawn into the game's fortunes in the summer of 1985. However inaccurate, an impression has developed that English football has made a rod for its own back by its misdirection of finances and by having a misplaced scale of financial priorities. Yet it is also clear that many clubs which have determined to invest their money in new buildings and stadium redevelopment (Chelsea, Wolves and Spurs, for instance) did so as a major financial gamble which, like other forms of capitalist investment (notably in transfer fees), might merely compound debts and interest payments without necessarily generating extra income. Whatever the purpose of the capital outlay, by the early 1980s the *interest* on the total accumulated debt of English league clubs was estimated at £25 million a year.[5]

The internal financial management of football clubs is, in most cases, peculiarly archaic, old fashioned and unsuited to the demands made of them. No better illustration can be provided than the data on the financial management of the clubs which became available in 1985. One major recommendation of the Chester report into the game's finances – and one which was accepted – was that the clubs should submit half-yearly financial returns, in July and January, to the Football League. The returns were to be entered on simple, standard forms (the likes of which would be familiar to and manageable by any competent treasurer of an amateur darts team).

Table 1.2   Financial reports: forms for League clubs

XYZ Club – Financial Report for Six Months Ended			
	Current six months		Previous six months
	%	£	%	£
1 Football Expenditure:			
(a) Remuneration of players			
(b) Remuneration of non-players			
(c) Match expenses			
(d) Hotel and travelling			
(e) Other direct expenses			
(f) Ground costs			
(g) Administration costs			
(h) Finance costs			
	———		———
	100%	———	100%	———
	———		———

2 *Football Income*
(a) League attendance
(b) League Cup attendance
(c) F.A. Cup attendance
(d) Other attendance
(e) Receipts from Football League
(f) Other receipts

3 *Commercial Income less Expenditure*
(a) Lotteries
(b) Sponsorship
(c) Other

4 *Transfer fees received (paid)*

_____   _____

_____   _____

5 *Profit(Loss)*

_____   _____

Club XYZ – Return of Liquid Position as at ....

	TOTAL £
Cash	
Investment	
Debtors	
	_____
(A)	
	_____

	TOTAL £	Due for Repayment within six months £
Bank Indebtedness		
Creditors		
Loans		
Forward commitments		
– for Capital		
– for Revenue	_____	_____
(B) (C)	_____	_____

If (C) exceeds (A) state how difference will be financed.

Source: Accountants Record, April 1985, p. 4.

By February 1985 it was reported that only twenty of the ninety-two clubs had fulfilled this requirement; most confessed that the exercise was beyond their facilities and those clubs which had done so had found the task difficult. Yet the questions asked were simple points about income and expenses, from the game and related income, and simple statements of the clubs' liquid position. Although the more alert members of the game instantly appreciated the fundamental significance of this data, it was generally ignored and emerged only in an article in a specialist accountants' journal.[6] In the winter of 1985 it thus became clear that football's finances were not merely chaotic in a cumulative and publicly admitted sense, but they were in a state of extraordinary confusion when we focus our attention on the clubs themselves. The very great majority of football clubs were simply incapable of accounting, at regular intervals, for their current state of income, expenses, liabilities and assets. The causes of this extraordinary state of affairs were doubtless varied. But it was none the less a shocking indictment of clubs and their governing bodies; a telling insight into their manifest inabilities to conduct themselves as efficient concerns. Once more, it needs to be reiterated that the game's endemic troubles were evident long before the disasters of 1985 brought them into finer focus.

The central problem facing football clubs is that of finance. Yet it is precisely in the area of financial management that the clubs have consistently shown themselves to be deficient. Not only do they appear to handle their own internal finances with a cavalier disregard for their main customers – the fans – but they are in danger of losing the financial lifeline cast in their direction by sponsorship. Many clubs would long since have disappeared without the extra income generated by local or national sponsorship. Apart from money which clubs receive to cover certain policing and improvements, they were able to attract more than £11 million from advertising, broadcasting fees and sponsorship, in 1985. Naturally enough (natural, that is, in a game dominated increasingly by competitive commercialism), this sum is not shared evenly between the clubs but is dispersed unequally between successful and less successful clubs.[7] There is pressure from humbler clubs for a more equitable redistribution of this income but this is unlikely to succeed. Even if it did, such redistribution would only shore up the collapsing finances of a number of clubs who are *already* incapable of providing adequate entertainment – on the field – adequate (and safe) stadium facilities and even a modicum of commercial good management. In a rapidly changing game there seems little attraction in shoring up the galaxy of ninety-two clubs which seek the subsidies of their bigger and more popular club mates, solely to perpetuate their existing inadequacies.

Sponsorship in football takes a number of forms. At a humble level, it might consist simply of a local company providing playing kit for an impoverished club. But this compares to the experience of the major clubs, adopted by international companies, who transform their colours and emblems, who bedeck their stadium (and players) in the company's *motif* and who oblige their players to jump through a variety of promotional hoops. Quite apart from these lucrative deals between sponsors and major clubs, the Football League has struck sponsorship deals – with milk and camera organisations – which, once more, break with established traditions and transform football's institutions into yet another commercial venture. Even then, the lion's share of the venture goes to the major clubs. Like sponsorship at the club level, it is a system which is designed to favour the big, successful clubs and to leave only the crumbs for the smaller and generally impecunious clubs. Thus the sponsorship system in operation until 1985 served to widen the gap between rich and poor.[8]

How could this be otherwise, in the very nature of the exercise? It is, at heart, a commercial venture designed to sell products and services – and that is scarcely feasible or attractive when done through struggling, unsuccessful or unpopular institutions – in this case football clubs. The problem, from the summer of 1985 onwards, is that the game itself has acquired such opprobrium, such public distaste, that it may become an unattractive 'product' for the marketing world. Which company wants, to put the matter simply, to be associated with a game which brought such terrible disasters upon its head? To a marketing world concerned above all else with image (and to which more fundamental issues like taste and even truth often seem alien), football has developed a flawed image which makes the task of salesmanship more difficult rather than easier. As long as the unpleasant aftermath of the two disasters linger on – the subject of continuing political altercation, legal enquiry and prosecution and of public curiosity – the more difficult it will be for the clubs and their organisations to lure sponsors, old and new, into football's corner. At the time of writing, the outcome is unpredictable but it seems likely that the shadows cast by the 1985 disasters will persist in darkening the game's financial security and future.

It is possible that those two terrible events will be the catalyst which will transform the game, simply by producing a fundamental financial crisis within the game and within a number of clubs. Once more, however, it needs to be said that the problems which the clubs refused steadfastly to tackle – notably the continuing survival of a structure of organisation and competition which belong to the earlier epochs of the game – will be solved in the most brutal and unsatisfactory fashion – by unplanned, indiscriminate 'market' forces. And the same point applies to the clubs' internal organisation; unable to keep their own financial house in order they are likely to be forced to do so, by external pressures, or simply collapse. For some, their problems may even be beyond redemption. Until 1985, the structure of the league (too big, too 'national' and a survival of an older generation of nationally popular football clubs) was able to totter along, from one season to another, by the internal cross-subsidies operating within the league and between the clubs. New laws and strict safety enforcements will almost certainly transform this pattern in the near future.

It is unquestionably true that football clubs do have legitimate financial grievances. The taxes levied on betting in football run at a current 42½ per cent; income to the Treasury which compares with a mere 8 per cent on horse-racing betting. Similarly, clubs feel unfairly penalised by VAT taxes on admission charges. But it has to be said that British governments – of any political line – are unlikely to make fiscal exceptions for an industry (football) which has consistently failed to demonstrate even a modest attempt to rationalise its own internal financial affairs, and which seeks financial and government help simply to allow the old clubs and the old organisations to continue much as before. To a government which has swung an effective axe at a number of primary industries, football's financial pleas seem less than persuasive. Moreover, in a broader British economy in which funds are in short supply, government is unlikely to reduce its income still further by reducing football's dues to the Treasury. Equally, the plea that other arts are heavily subsidised, and football ought therefore to be similarly treated, are unlikely to prove convincing in the glare of public attention paid to football's bizarre finances. To a British government anxious to prune Britain of its inefficiencies and to expect all institutions to measure up to standards of competitive international and traditional industry, there is little sense in guaranteeing football's traditional but now outdated methods and structures.

There are, to repeat, men within the game who are acutely aware of the game's financial plight and who have developed strategies to deal with it. Unfortunately, the organisational structure and the dogged-survivalism of many of the smaller and troubled clubs militates against the implementation of important rationalisations. There are important internal reforms which clubs could implement, notably reform of their own financial management. Similarly, it is thought possible that clubs would revise their shareholding systems to encourage wider public investment. But these – like sponsorship and gate income – depend ultimately on public confidence in the game and its future. In the summer of 1985 such confidence was at a low and debilitating ebb. The main thrust for income comes from sponsorship and media coverage. Yet in the aftermath of the disasters there are good commercial resources for advertisers (their goods and services beamed from the stadium into millions of homes via TV) to feel hesitant about associating themselves too closely with a faulty and uncertain 'product' – football. This is particularly the case with manufacturers of alcoholic drink, singled out as one of the main causes of football's troubles. It seems, at best, perverse to have a commercial link with a sport which specifically outlaws the product concerned. The man who, in 1985, was financial manager of Fulham FC made the following comment in the game's financial management:

> It is a combination of all the attributes which make any business in trade, industry, or a profession successful. Good housekeeping, a good product to sell, the correct marketing of the product, and the proper financing and capitalisation of the company.[9]

What is abundantly clear is that many of the English clubs come nowhere near this admirable ideal. And to make their problems worse, the events of 1985 have almost certainly worsened the climate in which they operate. Public (and political) confidence is an important ingredient in this – as in other financial and business matters. Once more, it seems likely that football clubs – and their fans – have made their own difficulties much worse.

So many of the game's problems are in fact the reverse side of the game's undoubted strengths; notably its strong historical traditions, and its commitment to long-established rituals of sporting and business activities. This is a point amply illustrated by the nature and conduct of football management.

Nothing illustrates more precisely the peculiar weaknesses of football than the recent history of club management. Indeed, the history of management in this one small and rather unimportant industry is a telling insight into the broader story of British attitudes towards business management in general. Professional, independent managers were virtually unknown in the game before 1945. Key decisions on all aspects of club management, and even team selection, were the preserve of the directors who were, overwhelmingly, no more qualified in such matters than the fans themselves. Managers were in effect the trainers who carried out the board's orders – but who carried the blame and responsibilities for mistakes and failures. This had begun to change by the mid-1950s; the increasing commercialism, the drive for decent wages for players and the growing attention from the media all demanded a more professional management of the teams and clubs. Directors began to demand professional managers – ex-players – who could guarantee success.[10] Not only was this impossible, for all but a handful, but the revolution of authority from directors to manager placed control in the hands of men who were untrained in any formal sense. They were, it is true, experienced and often successful ex-players. But their new role demanded other qualities and abilities: financial acumen, skilled man-management, sensitivity to the media (and fans) and a managerial flair – all of which were hard to find in the training they had had as players. As managers of business concerns, many – perhaps most – managers were no more competent than the directors. Yet all the time the financial consequences of their activities became more demanding and specialised. Although many were advised by professional administrators, the managers of football teams came to occupy an increasingly important role in their clubs financial well-being – or misfortunes.

The manager's relationship with the players changed substantially when, unlike in the days of maximum wages, each player negotiated his own salary and perks. Instead of managing a large club of poorly paid artisans, managers were now in charge of a small group of well-paid, in some cases lavishly paid, young men who were imbued with the belief that they are professionals. Yet this – like financial management – is something for which managers have had little training. Management of clubs, which were, in the rare prominent cases, multimillion pound commercial operations, was – and remains – in the hands of men with little but intuition, personal experience and a dogged determination to succeed. In this, it could be argued, football simply reflected the experience of wide areas of British management which specifically eschewed the concept of professional managerial training and vocational education. The crucial – and growing – importance of the manager can be measured by the speed and frequency of their dismissal, the litany of which is regularly recited to the public. But less frequently revealed are the financial ramifications of managerial failures or misjudgements; bad investments in players, excessive pay settlements and an inability to recruit outside funding, can leave a club burdened with long-standing difficulties long after a manager's departure. Of course, such major financial decisions were often shared by the board, but responsibility was and is generally shouldered by the manager.

So dire have financial problems become for a number of clubs that they have fallen into the hands of powerful benefactors; businessmen, rock stars and entrepreneurs anxious to salvage a tottering club and to attach their name to a publicly famous institution. Ironically, this is an old footballing pattern for the origins and early development of many clubs was often the work of successful local businessmen. Until the 1980s, it was virtually impossible to break into the local team's boardroom simply by financial clout. In recent years, however, it has become commonplace: 'Almost anyone with a million pounds to spare can become the chairman of a football club today.'[11] Clubs today see such a man as a fairy godfather, whose financial wand will transform loss into profit, failure into success. Often, such men are, by definition, astute self-publicists, with all the beneficial publicity likely to accrue to the club by his presence. Naturally enough, the publicity is not always as good as expected.

In a sense this recent phenomenon is a return to the original pattern, of the key role played by prominent local businessmen. The difference, however, is that today such men occupy a much more publicised role. Their activities in and outside their clubs are intimately scrutinised by the media, with all the consequent glare for the club itself. To many in the game, publicity is paramount. It is no longer enough merely to be successful; what is required is media coverage which will accentuate that success. Indeed, a number of men in football in recent years have been deemed failures not for their lack of footballing success but because their personal shyness or lack of interest has failed to generate sufficient publicity for the club. Self-made millionaires with an interest in (if not a knowledge of) the game seem ideal candidates for attracting both money – and free publicity.

Thus it was in the 1970s, when more and more clubs came to realise the seriousness of their problems that they began to change the traditional links with local businessmen and to seek or accept the dominance of nationally known figures. A rock star (Elton John) and a comedian (Eric Morecambe) led the way in the mid-1970s. As ever more clubs became manifestly unprofitable, the presence of a major guarantor of debts – or an investor – became crucial. In all four football leagues, prominent – in some cases flamboyant – businessmen took over certain clubs. Their arrival proved, in some cases, a mixed blessing, for their style of operations, the challenge they generally posed to the traditional order and manner of running club affairs often caused resentment and offence. It was not long before men experienced in the game registered unease about the course of events. The newly arrived saviours invested considerable sums in their clubs and were, not unnaturally, keen to see results. This has had the effect of accentuating the existing pressures for swift success. Yet the arrival of such men – their own personal success a guarantee of their financial wizardry – has served to underline the point already evident before their arrival and well rehearsed in this chapter – that what the clubs needed as much as finance itself was careful financial management. It is perfectly obvious, for example, that any amount of financial investment in certain clubs would be an exercise in financial folly, of throwing good money after bad, for these clubs' internal management (related to poor footballing performance) require much more than merely hard cash. If clubs are to survive – and it is hard to imagine how all ninety-two *can* survive within the existing extravagant structure of the four leagues – they will need more than cash. Hence the tendency to seek not only financial backers but a new generation of trained accountants – like Brian Dalton at Fulham – to put club affairs on a sound footing. In the last resort many investors realise that the central value in a football club is the real estate; land on prime urban sites which could be profitably redeveloped if the club failed.

In truth, the crisis facing the English national game was, in large measure, brought about by the clubs themselves. English football clubs remained extraordinary survivors of a former epoch; institutions whose nature, organisations and management were shaped in the formative years 1880–1914. The values which the clubs represented were similarly outdated, despite the undeniable accretion of modern commercial and sporting items. There were a host of other English institutions founded in precisely these years – industries, schools, churches, cinemas and homes – which have been greatly changed by the various forces of urban and industrial modernisation. Many have simply disappeared, bulldozed down in the process of urban renewal and population change which has transformed urban England since the 1950s. Many others have adapted themselves, more or less successfully, to new demands and tasks, while still others have been transformed into totally new institutions. Churches which are now mosques, chapels now used as warehouses – or homes – cinemas now entertaining thousands as bingo-halls – all these and more provide physical evidence of the transformation in English urban leisure in the past generation. Yet of all those Victorian and Edwardian institutions perhaps the most unchanging has been the professional football club. In most cases, among the smaller, poorer clubs, this point is amply illustrated by the physical plant; the terraces and stands which look more like museum pieces than a modern sports stadium.

In the summer of 1985 it became apparent that such quaint facilities were probably extremely dangerous. Other old institutions – the music halls, theatres and early cinemas – were obliged to modify and change their ways by earlier accidents and disasters. Now, decades after their heyday, the same pattern has unfolded for football clubs. And, as in other, earlier cases pressure for change has come from outside agencies – from public and political outrage confronted by unacceptable levels of institutional conservatism and an unquestioning commitment to old routines and institutions. The problems at Bradford's football ground illustrated not only the inadequacies of the physical facilities but the inner mentality of football's authorities – namely the league – which could, for so long, tolerate such conditions. Equally, it speaks for the amazing fidelity and pertinacity of the fans that they have for so long endured such conditions unflinchingly – except, of course, for those millions of fans who have simply quit the game for other pleasures. But if the clubs have remained unchanging, the players have been utterly transformed.

3 Feet of Clay: Modern Players

It has been argued so far that football has in many key respects remained unchanging; has failed to respond in a number of key institutional respects to new demands placed on the game. Indeed, it is a fundamental thesis of this book that the game's inability or unwillingness to change is the key to understanding its basic and growing problems. The structure of overall organisation, the internal management of the clubs and, most important of all, the mentality which has traditionally informed English football have all served to render the game brittle and unmoving. Moreover, this has been the case at a time of quite dramatic social change throughout British life in general and especially in the way people choose to spend their leisure time. This is not to claim, however, that the game has failed to change at all, for there are obviously a number of important differences in football which have made themselves felt over the past generation. But it is a game in which continuities, in form and conduct, far outweigh those changes. The appearance of change is quite powerful and nowhere more striking than on the fields of play, among the players.

Footballers have changed more dramatically than any other aspect of the modern professional game. They even look qualitatively different from their footballing forebears. Players at the end of the Second World War looked little different, in style and dress, from those of the 1920s. More recently, but especially from the 1960s, footballers began to respond to the stylistic and sartorial changes at work in society at large. The baggy shorts and loose-fitting shirts, the ponderous boots and the greased hairstyles were all dispensed with in favour of new, sleeker kit, and a personal appearance which reflected prevailing social trends. Each new male fad of the past twenty years was quickly reflected on the football field. Long hair became the first fashion, later joined by beards (a trend not really seen since the game's formative years in the late nineteenth century). This slowly gave way to the footballers' 'perm', as ever more professionals followed the vogue of having their hair curled; the end result was often more like a Pear's soap advertisement than the traditional short-back-and-sides of earlier players. But this too changed in time, giving way to the neatly trimmed haircuts and perfectly clipped moustaches so beloved of a new generation of young men throughout the western world in the mid-1980s.

Such changes – trivial and ephemeral as they unquestionably appear – are indicative of a much more fundamental transformation, for professional footballers have become more than mere sportsmen. They have been transmuted into 'stars' with all the commercial *éclat* and hype which accompanies such people. Of course, it is perfectly true that such stardom is the heady fate of only a small number of players, normally in the major clubs, but the style of the élite – itself substantially a reflection of broader cultural patterns – has proved consistently influential among their humbler brethren. In a sense, football is a game in which most players have determined to *look* like a star, whatever evidence to the contrary their footballing abilities might suggest. To understand this change, in appearance and substance, it is important to look at the players' history in the 1960s.

Until 1961 footballers were tied to universally applicable maximum wages. The legal and union struggle to defeat that system (itself a survival of old and, by 1961, grossly outdated industrial practices) was a turning point in the game's history. It unleashed economic forces, the ramifications of which could not have been fully predicted. The pre-1961 wage system was, without doubt, unjust, arbitrary and out of kilter with contemporary economic thinking and industrial relations. But what followed was, in some respects, no less bizarre. At a time of falling income (from smaller crowds) clubs faced a major escalation in players' wages. Clubs had to strive hard to keep their players by rewarding them handsomely and were consequently obliged to find extra income.[1] Many of their methods were simple (and simple-minded). Increasingly, however, clubs became acutely aware of their commercial potential – and limitations. But the players also began to appreciate the game's commercial potential. In large measure this was a result of the increased attention paid to the game – to its players and managers – by the press and, most importantly, by TV. From 1964 onwards *Match of the Day* began to give the game the detailed attention so familiar today. Subsequent technical innovations in film, camera, electronics and satellites (in addition to colour TV) inflated still further the attention to and interest in televised coverage of the game. At much the same time – and for reasons directly related to the spread and popularity of TV in British homes – newspapers began to compete ever more bitterly for their declining readership. The move of the popular press 'down-market' – the ever greater attention paid to trivial matters and the related inflation of sports coverage[2] – all served to bring football (and other games) an attention it had rarely enjoyed before.

The game had reached its initial peak of popularity a century ago, partly through the medium of the popular press operating within a largely literate urban workforce. But the events of the 1960s and 1970s were qualitatively different. First and foremost, the prime medium – TV – was visual, a tradition accentuated by the way even the newspapers personified the game, with lavish details about individual players and ever more space devoted to pictures. It was in keeping with the fundamental tradition of TV 'stars'. No matter how banal the task (weather forecasting), however routine the exercise (newsreading), TV was able to transmute performers into major and *national* personalities. Much the same was true of footballers. Among earlier generations of footballers, fame had, by and large, been a local phenomenon. Recognised in local communities, shops and pubs, travelling to and from the ground on the same buses as the fans, earlier generations of footballers were limited in their social life, and in their sporting prominence by their place within the distinctively local scale of things. Their wages, though generally better than the average industrial pay, were rarely high enough to raise them beyond the aspirations and the physical limitations of their immediate working-class peers – from whence most had come and among whom the ex-footballer invariably vanished. All this changed quite dramatically in the 1960s – though it is also true that there were hints of this change at an earlier date.

We must take care, though, not to exaggerate the degree to which footballers became national personalities. While undoubtedly true of the game's élite, it was decidedly not the case for the overwhelming majority of players whose toils (and rewards) in the lower leagues went largely unnoticed to anything like the degree of the stars. None the less even among humble teams, the expectations of players were greatly enhanced from the 1960s onwards, none more powerfully than the urge to strike lucrative pay deals. Similarly, the *style* affected by large numbers of footballers was dictated by the image of the footballer portrayed by TV and newspapers, and by those commercial interests which rapidly latched on to the game and its most prominent (i.e. commercial) stars. The end result was the emergence of the modern player; acutely conscious of his earning capacity, on and off the field, highly susceptible to lucrative and tempting offers and increasingly committed to a style of life and behaviour which was in many crucial respects new. It was a style which cut him off from his footballing forebears and, perhaps most important of all, from many of those working-class fans who formed the traditional bedrock of the game's supporters.

At its extreme, the development of the star system – the promotion of the footballer as a personality in his own right and removed from the game which had propelled him to fame – sometimes reached (and reaches) laughable extremes. Happy to promote virtually any product (a child's game, a local beer, even peanuts), the famous footballers lent their name, their faces and voices to the most incongruous of commercial ventures. Clearly it would be churlish to expect young men whose sporting careers are strictly limited to refuse to capitalise on their fame, and in this they are no different from other sportsmen and prominent personalities. But it was obvious that in many cases the selling of certain footballers' images took over from and transcended the very phenomenon which had made it all possible – the game of football.

The commercialisation of football stars was of a piece with the broader commercial transformation of the game itself. Throughout the late 1960s and 1970s football became a commercial venture to a degree and of a kind never previously experienced. Yet the mounting emphasis on the game's commercial importance took place when the fans began to desert the terraces in droves. It was one of those paradoxes which frequently characterised the history of sport that a game, whose value to the spectators was in indisputable decline, seemed to hold enhanced value to an ever broadening range of commercial interests.

There were in addition certain changes *within* the game which had a bearing on the relationship between fans and players. Numbers of clubs sought to cater for a 'superior' clientele by providing sumptuous private facilities – often taken up by business companies – of a kind totally unknown in the history of the game. But this trend took place at a time when humbler fans were left to endure the rigours of life on unimproved terraces. It was a game characterised by a host of sharp contrasts. The bulk of fans saw club money lavished unevenly on facilities for a favoured few. They also saw footballers whose rewards seemed to divorce them increasingly from the world of the ordinary fan. Clearly it is possible to exaggerate this divorce; some commentators have even sought the main explanation for football's declining fortunes in this divorce between players and fans. This phenomenon, however, is extremely difficult to evaluate not least because it is but one of a host of factors transforming the game over the past generation. The contrast between players and fans is sharp, notwithstanding the fact that many clubs, obliged to cut back their playing staff, have forced large numbers of players into unemployment – in August 1983 there were an estimated 250 unemployed professional footballers looking for work.[3] But the fans see not the unemployed player but those regularly in the public eye. And, whatever the economic reality, those players' earnings and lifestyle seem to be in sharp contrast to the world around them. This is particularly true when we consider the immediate urban environment in which the players work.

The more successful clubs – in Manchester, Liverpool and London – are still located on their early century sites; sites whose immediate social and economic hinterland has been so blighted in recent years. This is spectacularly the case in Liverpool where the local economy has disintegrated to a degree unusual even by contemporary English standards. We cannot assume (in the absence of hard evidence) that football fans have been disproportionately affected by local unemployment; that the game has suffered unduly because its traditional fans have been those most severely affected by unemployment. It is important to recall that attendance at football matches was in sharp decline *long before* the emergence of large-scale unemployment. None the less, it is worth stressing that the material well-being of the more prominent players (though clearly not all players) is in sharp relief to the material impoverishment of those communities to which the game has traditionally turned for its support and sympathy. It is again impossible to quantify but it is probable that this undeniable contrast – so extreme in the case of the game's élite – forms an irritant among certain fans. Players, who only a generation earlier had been closely tied to their supporters' communities and social levels, now find themselves removed into the rarified atmosphere of show business and stardom, earning in a few weeks money their fans could never hope to see after a year's labours. Once more, we need to place the discussion of players' wages within the broader debate about high income.

It has become a distinctively British (not simply English) political sentiment that high income earners are excessively paid (despite the obvious evidence to the contrary when comparisons are drawn with European or North American earnings). Senior public servants have their own top pay tribunal, and governments of conflicting policies have generally found it difficult to reward senior officials with high pay awards without facing political and public disquiet. Indeed, in the summer of 1985 Mrs Thatcher's decision to implement hefty awards for top-salaried officials caused a major political outcry. Of course, this was a specific political problem but the response to it (led by newspaper editors and columnists not unfamiliar with the problems of high earnings) is the most important evidence for the case outlined here. Clearly there is a world of difference between public antipathy to massive salaries for public servants, and the public's response to salaries gained in the free market. And nowhere is it freer and more spectacularly rewarding than in show business, of which football has become a part. Even here, it is likely that there is public cynicism about the levels of earnings of prominent stars, albeit a cynicism tinged by envy. The sense that no one is really worth salaries measured upwards of £100 000 is too often repeated to be merely an isolated sentiment. It would be very difficult to link directly such vague unease with the unquestionably widespread opposition to high pay settlements for public servants but it is possible that both are aspects of the same, general, feeling that high income is unnecessary.

This is a sentiment which has been expressed by politicians of all persuasions. Among Labour politicians – and union bosses – the issue of high salaries can be guaranteed to produce squeals of outrage. Even among their Conservative opponents, and despite the evidence to the contrary, it is often thought that excessive salaries are unwise if only because politically unpopular. And such salaries have become *increasingly* unpopular because they seem to flaunt excessive material wealth in the face of millions of unemployed and low income groups. Here we return to the nub of the problem; that high income, and the lifestyle which normally goes with it, is a socially divisive issue in a society for long sorely taxed by social divisions. What then are we to make of footballers – if only a minority of them – whose earnings place them firmly (if only temporarily) among the nation's élite, but whose traditional communities of support have been so afflicted by depression? However difficult it may be to illustrate the alienating effect this has upon the fans, it is hard to deny its existence as a social and economic fact.

What compounds the cynicism of many fans is the belief that modern footballers, and the games they play in, are not as good as earlier generations. There is, quite obviously, no way of proving this feeling. Even the consumer test, of declining attendances, is an inadequate indication because as we have seen repeatedly throughout this book, the determining social and economic context of the game is utterly different today from its heyday in the late 1940s. Indeed, when compared to the decline of cinema, or rugby league, soccer has suffered less severely.[4] None the less, the feeling that the game and the players have changed – for the worse – is a ubiquitous theme in responses to social surveys over the past decade.[5] Similarly, older men, disillusioned with the game, frequently complain that the game and its practitioners are inferior, a complaint also commonly expressed by ex-managers and players.[6] It is interesting that this view generally comes from older men, the very group whose attendance has fallen away most dramatically from the game.[7] Indeed, this feeling has brought about a shift in formal training strategies, with the FA sanctioning an emphasis on individual skills and virtuosity rather than rigid coaching systems. The disillusionment of older fans is, to a degree, inevitable; how could younger fans have the experience – in terms of their years – to adopt such a comparative judgement?

It is, naturally enough, extremely difficult to know what importance to attach to the disillusionment with the game and its players (though it has to be said that the *major* factor in driving away fans is not the players but the behaviour of the fans themselves).[8] There are, however, certain areas worth speculating about. Again, we need to consider the impact of TV. It is perfectly reasonable that TV coverage – of football or any other sport or event – should expect to extract maximum entertainment from it. In the case of football this has involved editing games down to fit into the appropriate programme time and format. Most of the football seen on TV is in the form of highlights (though not even the most skilful of editors can sometimes hide a poor game). This is done quite simply by eliminating the dull, boring, less entertaining parts. With the exception of those rare games shown in their entirety, TV coverage thus has the effect of showing the best and eliminating the worst. To put the matter so boldly is not to criticise TV football. But it is clear that televised football is unusual to the degree that it is selected for its entertainment value. It remains true that players' mistakes or shortcomings – like their more spectacular displays of skill or scoring – are often kept in for their entertainment value. There is, in

a sense, a cruel and remorseless quality to TV coverage, for it will
spot, enlarge and repeat in slow motion isolated errors and the
exceptional act, be it of folly, aggression or brilliance. Players often
complain that their slips are magnified and remembered even in an
otherwise unblemished game. But this is merely the price which
famous people – in sport as in politics – must pay for their fame. To
the extent that TV has made many of the players into personalities
and stars, it also has the power to make them look ridiculous.

For our purposes, TV coverage of football has done much more
than alter the status and role of the players, for it has also created
quite different expectations of their performances and abilities. To
earlier generations of fans or observers, footballers' talents were
appreciated by simply watching football, reading newspaper
reports or listening to gossip about the game. Since the mid-1960s,
however, many more people – upwards of 6 million each week – are
privy to the footballers' achievements and failures, their skills and
blunders, simply by watching TV. Moreover, this mass TV audience
is carefully coached in its appreciation of the game's finer – or cruder
– points by a bevy of experts, normally ex-footballers, whose
commentaries on the highlights and the slow motion replays
provide guidelines for the audience's critical appreciation. This is
not to say that the TV audience meekly accepts all that is said by the
experts, but rather that TV coverage involves much more than the
transmission of televised sport into the home.

The main point to be stressed is that over the past twenty years
people have come to expect much more of the game and of its
players. First, watching football at home is much more comfortable
than watching it, in mid-winter, at a stadium. This was crucially
illustrated when live coverage of games resulted in a significant fall
in the attendance at the game itself. More significantly, however,
the fans have become accustomed, over twenty years, to seeing a
form of sanitised football – games from which the boredom has been
purged and in which entertainment has been selected, inflated and
endlessly repeated. It is within this, utterly changed, context of the
game's recent history in England that fans – armchair and terrace –
air their views about players' skills or weaknesses and about the
general decline in footballing standards and entertainment.
Furthermore, there is now (in the mid-1980s) much more football for
fans to watch. Television is able, thanks to satellites and modern
electronics, to bring highlights from games around the world into
the home at weekly intervals. Thus local players find themselves

compared not only with their peers at home but with their competitors wherever the game is played. Once more, such highlights are transmitted for their entertainment value. But in the process they become an important yardstick against which more local performers can be assessed.

It takes no leap of the imagination to see that the reality of a Saturday game, often played in adverse conditions (and sometimes viewed in worse), is a qualitatively different experience. No player can perform at the peak of performance for a whole game; highlights by definition ignore the mundane and the tedious. Players on the field cannot always play as they appear to play in selected highlights, often to the frustration of the spectators. Moreover, there is a case to make that televised highlights have also transformed the fans' patience and judgement. Much of a game's basic attraction is the development – often slow and painstaking – of moves and manoeuvres, the careful and considered tactical give and take which is often less spectacular than the more eye-catching incidents. Thus to large numbers of spectators much of the activity in a game can easily be viewed as boring or unattractive.

This is not to say that there is no tedium in the modern game; there clearly is. Much of that tedium is itself partly a result of tactical changes, which were developed in response to the escalating commercial importance of winning (or at least of not losing) and the three points for a win. Furthermore, in the perfection of tactical play, television and film have become crucial in giving managers and coaches a permanent insight into their opponents' play. But the key point to be reiterated here is that expectations of the players' performances and abilities have been utterly transmuted by the coming of regular TV coverage. Nor is this the sole consequence of televised football for there is a great deal of evidence to suggest that players have indeed altered their performance under the transforming stare of TV cameras.

Players and certain fans seem to be as one in their response to cameras. Television provides the opportunity for projecting the personality through the most exaggerated and often bizarre gestures and forms of behaviour. Players who had in the past restricted their gestures and mannerisms – of despair or elation – to the paying spectator, now direct their antics towards the cameras. It is extremely difficult to analyse this phenomenon, if only because the evidence tends to be visual, fleeting and with little from the past against which to contrast it. Old news-reels of football matches, though revealing that players did indeed congratulate each other and show signs of annoyance or joy, also suggest that players' responses were much more restrained. Whether this was a function of a greater personal and collective discipline is hard to say, but it is easy to understand how older fans often view the histrionics of modern players as a sign of declining discipline. In truth, players – like others around them – simply behave differently from their forebears. And in part that difference relates to the contagious influence of television coverage. Certain forms of exaggerated behaviour have become *de rigueur* among most professional players. Obviously, they watch each other on the field, but they also watch most other successful teams on TV. A generation ago, the more excessive forms of players' exuberance – players mobbed for scoring, feigned and utterly deceptive injuries – were widely thought to be an alien expression; more suited to the 'hot' temperaments of Latin America and southern Europe. Yet today precisely the same outbursts – so disruptive of the game and so diversionary from the issues at hand – have become regular and unexceptional features of the English game. Attempts to regulate or ban them have so far failed.

One plausible explanation might be an issue which has run like a refrain through this chapter; the heightened commercialism of the game. There is quite simply more at stake than merely a game. Indeed, the players' wages are generally determined by their successes; the more successful a team, the bigger the crowd, the higher the wages. And at the upper reaches of the game, success in major national competitions opens the door – until 1985 that is – to lucrative European games. It would be wrong to suggest that players' wild enthusiasm at moments of success are uniquely determined by financial consideration. But to overlook the fact of the commercial importance of winning (and scoring) would be to ignore a major element in the make-up of the modern professional game.

More troublesome still perhaps than the predictable excitement of the players is the thorny question about whether their sporting behaviour has deteriorated. Again, the evidence is difficult to assess. Like most forms of 'deviant' behaviour, footballing misdemeanours depend to an extraordinary degree on the vagaries of changing policies and the variations between referees. One referee might swear at a player, another might send off a player for using the same language. Similarly, if football's authorities determine to clamp down on certain forms of players' behaviour, the data on bookings and sending-off will change dramatically. There is clear evidence, however, that players do behave differently and are not unashamed to indulge in 'ungentlemanly' behaviour. Recent research, using players' and managers' autobiographies and public statements (evidence we need to treat with a degree of caution), has amply illustrated the degree to which footballers are encouraged to misbehave and to flout the laws – trying all the time not to be caught.[9] The concept of a 'professional foul' has entered into the English vernacular[10] to describe a form of behaviour which, if technically illegal, is justified in terms of the end result. In this, if in nothing else, the modern professional is worlds removed from his sporting forebears.

The very concept of 'sporting' denoted an attitude of fairmindedness and a willingness to concede defeat to opponents. It was a quintessential Victorian and Edwardian social value, originating in the public schools but rapidly spreading throughout British (and indeed imperial) life by the First World War. In the early days of modern football, the public school pioneers of the game even rejected the initial efforts to award a penalty; it presumed that one player had deliberately fouled another player. Equally, in that rich fictional literature, in magazines and books written for and about the English public schools, the 'bounder', the 'cad' was often portrayed as the boy who simply failed to abide by the rules of the game. 'Playing the game' involved much more than simply committing oneself utterly to the interests of the team; it also meant abiding by the rules. This could even involve conceding a point to opponents if one knew a transgression had taken place but the referee had not spotted it. One of the last survivals of this phenomenon is when a cricketing batsman, knowing he has touched the ball and been caught, will 'walk'; will effectively give himself out, contrary to the umpire's judgement.

We need not romanticise this matter for it was at heart a code of ethics, devised at a particular period and for a specific purpose. As times changed so did the attachment to the code and the ethics. Long before the First World War, the amateur world of football, dominated by founding public school fathers, was deeply and increasingly unhappy with the conduct of the professional game. The criticisms made of professional football showed all the elements of more recent judgements. But it was a sign of changing values – in sport and in society at large – that the older values and their proponents were represented as archaic and irrelevant. What produced this transformation was, at heart, the commercial and professional developments within the game. What we have seen in the past generation is a remarkable escalation and exaggeration of a process that goes back to the early part of the century.

It would be quite wrong to suggest that the old sporting ethic has utterly disappeared. None the less modern players are much more likely to be influenced by quite different values of play. They are, first and foremost, professional athletes dedicated to winning.[11] They have to operate within the determining rules of their sport. But they bend those rules, gain advantage by ignoring them, blatantly disregard them at critical moments (with a 'professional foul') and put the arbitrator of the rules (the referee) under extraordinary personal pressure to gain advantage or dispute a ruling. The end result can be seen at most modern games, in which players will automatically dispute what they know to be right, will sometimes hurt a fellow player to stop him (though this is much worse in non-professional rugby), and will bellow and surround the referee when offended by his judgements. Nor are these modern trends restricted to professionals but can be seen at any amateur game. Players have, furthermore, been instructed to conduct themselves in this way by managers and trainers; to seek to gain personal and team advantage at all costs. And the development of this constant challenge to the game's rule of law has, without doubt, produced a different type of behaviour among the players.

This is not to say that older generations of players were less tough or more concessionary towards opponents, but merely that the modern professional player has taken the process to its logical extreme. To older commentators, influenced by a qualitatively different approach to the game (less intent on winning at all costs, less outraged at the prospect of defeat), the modern game often seems like an exercise in ungentlemanly conduct. And, in a fashion, it is. The modern professional player – all of whom have grown up in a footballing world increasingly dominated by commercial interests – is unlikely even to be *familiar* with the concept of gentlemanly conduct (except in so far as it is part of the popular vernacular). For many observers, however, this is a matter of deep regret; an irrefutable sign that the game and its players have been corrupted by the excessive dominance of commercial considerations. For many others, it is a process which has purged the game of its enjoyment and its fun. For critics who feel this way about the game – among whom are to be counted numbers of sports reporters who have seen changes over the past few decades – the blame is generally directed at the players. This is not so surprising since they are the basis of the professional game itself. They are the people who attract – or repel – the spectators and who personify (to an increasing degree) the game itself.

For many fans and observers the problems of football have come to be identified with the players. Players have become, for many of their former admirers, idols with feet of clay. To others, the players' behaviour represents some of the worst aspects of changing social values. Yet we need not reject these criticisms entirely by insisting on the caveat that the players are themselves victims of powerful commercial forces which can discard them as readily as adopt and pamper them. Players, like the game they personify, have been changed by commercial interests into personalities which often owe little to their basic abilities – as footballers. They are, after all, only footballers. Many of their problems – and of the unrealistic expectations demanded of them – is that this central and basic fact is all too often forgotten.

4 Fanatics

Fanatical support for a particular football team has been a characteristic feature of the game since its inception, in its modern form, a century ago.[1] Football is not alone in this for there are numerous games, in Britain and abroad, whose success and even survival depend to a marked degree on the unswerving loyalty of supporters. American baseball teams, Aussie-rule football teams, Welsh rugby union teams – the list is long and worldwide – and all have similar patterns of passionate support in their local communities. Such support, naturally enough, fluctuates enormously but even when a team's fortunes are at a low ebb they can generally rely on a small nucleus of supporters whose commitment to the team is total and unwavering. In the case of modern football such support has been the major force in providing the game with its essential financial life-blood. But football support goes well beyond merely attending a match and helping to finance a club, for it has, throughout the history of the modern game, often been a form of attachment not merely to a particular team but to all that the team stands for; locality, religion and local way of life.[2]

Generations of men go through adult life supporting the local team of their childhood; a football team can thus represent a formative period or episode in a person's life and remain a major preoccupation despite the passing of time and despite distance. Millions of people take the sporting passions of their early years to the distant relocations of adult life. Furthermore, the modern coverage of sports on TV and the projection of sport around the world has generated enthusiasm for particular games, teams or players in the far corners of the world. People can now claim to be a Liverpool or Manchester United fan yet may never have left their homeland, thousands of miles distant from those clubs. But the development, in very recent years, of a new and qualitatively different type of fan, or rather the development of new and generally unacceptable forms of behaviour among some of those fans, represents a marked shift in the nature of support for football. Inevitably these new forms of support and supporters (often dismissed as being not 'real' fans) have aroused a fierce hostility not only among more 'traditional' supporters but, no less important, in the media and among politicans. Long before the Brussels disaster, the very connotation of what constitutes a football fan had been utterly transmuted by the emergence of the football 'hooligan'.[3] And yet it is important to consider the more long-term nature of support and supporters before we can fully understand those changes which have come to typify and disfigure the modern English game.

The traditional folk customs of football were marked by local, often parochial, attachments and were generally sporting disputes which subsumed territorial and parish rivalries. Often, these games provided an opportunity for local youths and young men to settle old scores against rival groups or individuals.[4] But the emergence of the modern game inside the early nineteenth-century public schools saw the development of that ethos of competitiveness and attachment to team which laid the foundations for much of what was to follow later in the century. The development of modern games of football within the public schools, part of the process of disciplining those previously chaotic schools, hinged upon the codification and regulation of the games, the establishment of a hierarchy of authority and the cultivation of widespread support among players and other boys for the success of their teams. Public school players were encouraged to give their all not only for the team but also for the 'house' it represented and, in inter-school games, for the name of the school itself. It was part of the ambition – and success – of public school house and headmaster that they cultivated these fierce attachments to team, house and school which, by the late century, had become characteristic of public school life but which were in fact quite new.[5]

This sense of loyalty, of unquestioning commitment, remained among the most durable legacies of life at a public school and which held together diverse bodies of men in an attachment to their former schools. Throughout, the agency of competitiveness had been basic to maintaining the support of boys to their teams. Competitions between houses and schools became increasingly sophisticated, with leagues, knock-out tournaments, major public occasions and the attendant awarding of colours, trophies, pennants, medals and awards of all descriptions. These artifacts of success (and failure) were often ends in themselves which, in many late century schools where athleticism began to triumph over scholarship, boys aspired to as the ultimate achievement of their school days. Many schools came to value sporting prowess before scholastic achievements not only among boys at the schools but, just as important, among old boys at Oxford and Cambridge. This was, of course, a complex process with enormous variations to the general pattern, but the end result was the development, in public schools and at Oxford and Cambridge, of the cult of manly athleticism to the exclusion of other ambitions and achievements.

This athleticism, however, did not always demand that commitment to victory at all costs which we associate with modern games. On the contrary, it often mattered not that the game or the event be won, but that the athletes should compete with the greatest of vigour and should conduct themselves to the credit and honour of their team, house or school. Winning was not always the main object of this sporting cult. None the less, public school athleticism consciously used competition – cultivated a sense of selfless competitiveness among pupils – as a basic ingredient in the transformation of the school, and the ethos which they generated. It was also a competitiveness which became increasingly nationalistic and xenophobic towards the end of the century, and the competitive attachment to country and to patriotic values was of great importance in that jingoistic spirit which suffused public schoolrooms in the Boer War and in 1914.[6]

All this may seem a long way removed from the world of the working-class football fan but in fact the links were direct and influential. The structure of competitiveness which emerged in public school games was ideally suited to the task of encouraging sporting endeavour and community-based sporting loyalties in the last twenty years of the nineteenth century. First the new compulsory schooling system of those years was developed and shaped by men who were themselves products of, or influenced by, public school educational and athletic ideals. Understandably, board schools throughout urban England were swift to adopt forms of competitive athleticism, notably football, which in many key respects mirrored the sporting patterns and ethos of their social superiors. Schools in working-class communities had their own teams, houses, competitions and competitive games with other city schools. Similarly, the game rapidly took root in adult working-class life, emerging from local trades unions, factories (or sections of a factory), churches and a number of other institutions, where it was encouraged by men of substance and influence and who had often acquired a taste for sporting commitment and were keen to pass it on to their less fortunate countrymen. From the first, the spread of plebeian football was aided by a competitive instinct. Indeed, this was true of a number of other popular cultural forms – choral singing and brass bands, for example – which thrived on competitive involvement. Local choirs, bands and football teams became famous not merely for being excellent exponents of their art and skill but for being better than, and beating, their rivals.

In the case of football, the competitive structure of the game, already developed within the public schools, quickly thrived in working-class communities, particularly in schools and factories. By the 1880s, all had their own leagues and knock-out competitions, with their own plethora of awards and emblems of victory. The whole process was completed by the rapid development of commercial and professional interests which transformed the game into the one familiar today. But it would be wrong to assume that competitiveness was a function of the development of professional, capitalist and commercial interests; they took what was already in existence and gave it a more overtly commercial structure. What they were able to achieve was the acceleration of local and regional competitiveness within the new national framework of professional and semi-professional football.

The teams which developed into the modern professional clubs derived their support and backing from specific local communities; a particular group of workers, a specific factory or church membership.[7] But this was inevitably inflated when, moving into a new custom-built stadium, they began to lay claims to a much broader community of support and commitment. Much of course depended on the nature of the community. Smaller towns could direct their interest to one particular club, while in the bigger cities a number of clubs effectively divided up their footballing constituency into rival factions of supporters. Much of that process was accidental – a simple process of urban settlement and the attraction of specifically local support to the nearest club. Often, the process was more complex and reflected not merely geography but that confusion of social forces which created a mosaic of urban loyalties and commitments throughout mainland Britain. Few loyalties were more potent than religion. Certain clubs, reflecting the nature of their immediate origins and social geography, were religious clubs; Protestant or Catholic in varying degrees of intensity – though never as intense in England as it was, from the first, in the Glaswegian sectarianism of Celtic and Rangers.[8] Yet even in such cases geography was important, for plebeian catholicism, substantially an Irish and therefore immigrant phenomenon in

the nineteenth century, often followed specifically local, geographic
lines

Thus by the early years of this century, in broad outline, the
passion of football fans was shaped and informed by local origins
and loyalties. Teams and clubs represented the attachment of fans to
locality and local community, in competition with other rival, albeit
neighbouring, communities. It was in a sense almost a return to the
pre-modern, traditional world where social life had been
determined not by any sense of belonging to, or fondness for, the
nation at large, but to the locality and the parish. For centuries
England had been a mosaic of local communities fused into a nation
by the agency of law. Only in the nineteenth century with the
development of a recognisably modern bureaucratic state, did a
sense of nationhood begin to replace attachment to local
community.[9] Yet in the flowering of popular culture, from the 1880s
to 1914, what we can see is the revival of that specifically *local*
sequence of passion and attachments which came to dominate
public expression of sporting enthusiasm. But unlike the pre-
modern world, these local attachments were now urban, primarily
industrial – and could now be expressed in an organised form, on the
terraces of football grounds.

These local passions were readily paraded throughout the length
and breadth of the country thanks to the travelling football fans, on
cheap excursion trains, who made their collective presence felt in
the towns and cities of opposing teams. It was, by and large,
innocent and harmless enough. There were, it is true, periodic
complaints of drunkenness, of foul language and generally high
spirits among the bands of travelling fans (who tended by and large
to be young). But such unruliness was generally no worse than
other periodic eruptions in urban life (notably on Saturday nights),
and often much better than the rowdiness to be found among young
men at the seaside resorts in the summer.[10] Nevertheless, there was
an unquestioned element of territorial and local rivalries involved;
of asserting the superiority of one town (or part of town) over a
neighbour or rival; of asserting the supremacy of provincial over
metropolitan life and the flaunting of parochial achievements in the
case of a local 'Derby'. Indeed, the development of the idea of a
'Derby' – its name directly derived from the pre-modern folk games
of football – is itself testimony to this very process – to the flowering
of vociferous and well-publicised attachments to localities and to the
clubs they spawned and sustained.

In all this, the press was crucial for it skilfully played open the passions of football fans. Specialised sports newspapers and the sports pages of national pages were instrumental in encouraging the spread of footballing interest (among a nation where mass literacy had firmly established itself). But the local press played an even more important role in placing great emphasis upon the minutiae of local teams and their players.[11] The press constantly whetted the appetite for the progress of local teams; 'stars' were substantially created by the press coverage, and praise and blame were liberally allocated to the heroes and villains of the local teams. Ultimately, of course, the game prospered – or sagged – depending on the quality of football played. But it was abundantly clear, by the early years of this century, that the *interest* in the game, the knowledge among its fans about the details of teams' and players' performances, the exaggerated and passionate commitment to this team and that – in fact all of those features of the game which became its dominant characteristics through the twentieth century – came to depend to a marked degree upon their presentation in the press. This is not to claim that football support was merely a conjuring trick played by a self-interested press. But it is true that many of the game's most salient social characteristics had been deeply influenced and exaggerated by the press. Whatever the cause, there could be no denying the passionate attachment to local football teams by millions of Englishmen (primarily working men) by the early years of this century.

The broad patterns of support – and behaviour – established among English fans by 1914 continued in much the same vein in the inter-war years. Even in times of great economic distress, and often *especially* in those communities most severely damaged by the slump (the North-East for instance), the passionate commitment to local teams continued unabated. It seems that the local teams – when successful – often became the mascot and symbol of local pride in a community in which there was little else to take pride. Times of austerity seemed to give local football fans an added attachment to their teams, despite the fact that in the genesis of the modern game what had shaped the initial popular attachment to the game had been *improving* material conditions among certain sections of working men. Furthermore, the wretchedness of urban and industrial conditions in the 1920s and 1930s did not seem to spark off trouble among the fans. Urban deprivation, unemployment and a general lack of material prospects did not, as far as we can tell, create

those troublesome organisations and flurries of disturbances among
local fans which numbers of modern commentators have detected in
recent years. If it is true that modern urban/economic troubles lie at
the heart of the recent disturbances among football fans, this seems
not to have been the case in the inter-war years.

Much the same was true in the immediate post-war years; years of
extraordinary and unparalleled support for football, and other
popular leisure pursuits. The late 1940s saw football fans attending
matches in unprecedented numbers. Yet these were years infamous
for their austerity (an austerity all the more difficult to tolerate
because it followed the privation and hardships of wartime). Once
more, austerity seemed to be the stimulant for the gathering of
massive (and peaceable) football crowds. And the same was true, as
we have seen, for cinema attendance and seaside trips.[12]
Throughout the late 1940s and the 1950s, when numbers at football
matches had begun to decline dramatically, football crowds were
recognisably similar to those crowding the stadiums throughout the
century. In social origins, sex and peaceableness, the football fan
remained a relatively unchanging type – notwithstanding the
existence of obvious exceptions (notably in Glasgow). There were
incidents of disorderly behaviour in the late 1940s and 1950s, but
they were few and were unusual. When English fans began to
misbehave in an increasingly obvious and frequent way, in the
1960s, it was clear that many of the old rituals and structures of
support had themselves begun to change. Indeed it was common,
when the question of football hooliganism began to be discussed in
the 1960s, to assume that it was a function of prosperity; of
privileged youths, with more money than sense, wantonly being
disruptive. Such arguments began to take on a new meaning by the
1970s.

In the past twenty years changes have transformed English fans
to a degree, and at a pace, which has proved utterly bewildering to
those observers and fans of the game accustomed, over many
decades, to viewing English football as an unchanging and ever
predictable landmark on the English urban landscape. The pattern
of support for the English game has, since the 1960s, changed quite
markedly and in the process the nature of the English fan has
changed, or rather, to be more accurate, new groups of fans have
developed which seem to owe little in style or behaviour to the
traditional provenance of the English fan. The groupings, the
organisations, the clothing and emblems, the chants and the

conduct of certain sections of English football fans are utterly different from anything known to the English game before the 1960s. It is perfectly true, and as we have already seen, that die-hard fans throughout the past century have roamed urban England in recognisable groups with their team colours and favours and bringing an element of noisy boisterousness to their journeys and the games. But this was, to repeat, a qualitatively different phenomenon from the behaviour of modern fans.

The terminology used to describe this modern phenomenon is itself indicative of this change. The word 'hooligan' has been appropriated to describe sections of English football fans. Indeed it is often used uniquely in relation to football. Since the 1970s the media has assumed that when they speak of 'hooligans' the reading and viewing public will know that they are referring to a certain underclass of football fans. This 'hooligan' element does, however, have direct links to the older, traditional base of support for the game.

Empirical data, collected from arrests of certain fans, shows that the very great majority of them are young men in labouring jobs – or unemployed – evidence which has been confirmed by detailed local studies.[13] It is true that violence among fans (against rivals, on property, against players) had punctuated earlier epochs of the game.[14] But disorderly conduct among fans went into decline after 1945, only to revive on an apparently ever increasing scale from the 1960s.

It is not the case that the growing alarm about football fans' behaviour since the 1960s is merely another example of a 'moral panic' periodically unleashed by the media, transforming insignificant matters into major matters of public concern. It may seem a bizarre point to make in the aftermath of Brussels, but the problem of hooliganism among fans is a real one; the behaviour of certain sections of fans has changed, has become more violent, more abusive (and more racist). At the very time when more prosperous – often more 'respectable' – working men began to find other leisure pursuits more attractive, a 'rougher' element, of younger less privileged fans, were able to take over key sections of certain crowds. Once established, their assertive and generally offensive behaviour drove out those fans who did not like or share this style of support and behaviour. Increasingly, certain sections of many football grounds became the effective monopoly and preserve of certain groups and gangs. (Some of those gangs pride themselves in

their stylish and costly dress, their members generally being in
well-paid work.) Often these groups adopted names from their
particular territory; they were, in effect, gangs within the broader
body of local supporters. As such they often sought to confirm and
assert their territorial identity not only by organised chanting (much
of it abusive and racist), but also by wearing particular emblems,
clothes or adopting their own distinctive sartorial style. Subjected to
detailed – and often inflammatory media coverage (newspapers
were not above fuelling such behaviour by giving money and drink
in local pubs in order to secure a good story)[15] – such young men
found a perfect stage on which they could rehearse their self-
conscious and exaggerated displays of violent masculinity. And the
more outrageous the behaviour, the wider the gulf became between
the football gangs and the rest of football supporters.

The situation was abetted by many of the physical changes in the
stadiums themselves. More respectable fans, no longer prepared to
tolerate the persistently dreadful physical conditions in many of the
nation's football grounds, retreated to plusher conditions in the
seated sections, though in some cases the thugs have invaded the
seats. This had the effect, in conjunction with the factors already
mentioned, of isolating still further the wilder fringes of the fans.
And to compound this process to a greater degree, more rigorous
policing methods, designed to isolate and identify potential trouble-
makers, segmented the crowds into distinctive groups; to isolate
locals and visitors (for their own safety) and to be able to scrutinise
the behaviour of those gangs which are physically obvious, and to
intervene against troublesome individuals if and when the occasion
arose.

This process took on a great deal of sophisticated electronic
scrutiny, with TV cameras and videos strategically installed to
pinpoint and record wrong-doers. Similar tactics were employed in
transit, as armies of policemen marshalled, patrolled and escorted
visiting fans to and from railway stations and car parks. Some of the
consequent sights were bizarre in the extreme with large gangs of
remarkably dressed fans, banners and abuse swirling through the
air, flanked by mounted police and headed by heavily shielded
police vehicles. It often looked more like a march of the National
Front, or of a contentious parade in Ulster, than a procession of fans
to a local football ground. While such extraordinary preparations
were, by the early 1980s extremely effective in controlling and
containing football fans (there was rarely major trouble at the bigger

grounds and clubs), there were many people, fans and non-fans, who found the whole affair distasteful in the extreme. While it is inevitably enough difficult to gauge, it seems likely that such sights helped to reinforce the disillusionment which many fans felt with the game. The game which millions held in such regard, and for which they held such proud memories, was sullied by (relatively small gangs of) modern fans whose behaviour, language, dress and general presence seemed a denial of all that the game represented.

Despite the very effective policing of the fans, tranquillity could never be absolutely guaranteed. There were occasions when clubs and police were caught totally unprepared by acts of spontaneous or carefully orchestrated acts of fan's violence. Even before the Brussels affair, the 1984–5 English season had been scarred by a number of such incidents, with some extraordinary acts of violence, drunkenness and in one case a fatality. There were, not surprisingly, growing numbers of fans whose loyalty to the game was strained to the limits by other fans, and who felt that the risks and the general unpleasantness were more than they could bear. It is obviously enough impossible to calculate such sentiment in terms of the numbers of paying fans lost to the game. But it is not too fanciful to see how, at the very least, it served to accentuate the widening disillusionment among fans (and non-fans) with the game of football.

Throughout the 1970s, the phenomenon of football hooliganism began to attract increasing attention, notably from sociologists who scrutinised the behaviour and composition of fans (who were so often dismissed as 'untypical'). But much of that research – as popularised through the media – was dismissed because it seemed so conspicuously at odds with what could be seen, heard and experienced at football grounds.[16] The danger is that the rejecting of important research evidence and the adoption of a 'commonsensical' approach to the problem may lead to ill-informed treatment and policies. It was precisely this response which characterised most of the political and press response to the Brussels disaster. Indeed, the Prime Minister specifically dismissed that corpus of research into football fans with the assertion that what was needed was action not words. Treatment without proper diagnosis is scarcely an attractive or promising line of development – in this or any other social problem. Yet the immediate political response to Brussels was to set in train a sequence of events which may well *ignore* the source of football's problems by concentrating on curbing certain forms of behaviour.

We now know a great deal about troublesome fans, about their social origins, local and family backgrounds and educational attainment. Yet to provide an identikit picture of the typical football fan (or rather those involved in the troubles) does not in itself explain why such men should find so perfect a venue for their activities at and around football grounds. Equally it needs also to be stressed that not all (presumably *not even a large proportion*) of youths of similar circumstances choose to join in the activities. There is, to put it crudely, nothing *inevitable* that compels such youths to become violent football fans.

What is important is the pressure of cultural emulation; the powerful social pressures to conform to certain forms of behaviour and to follow the influential lead of prominent local youths and styles. There is a sense in which the popular cult of the 'gang', however loosely defined, has come to play a major role in the broad cultural attachment to certain football teams. In the process, though it may seem odd to say it, football is not important save as an occasion for the rituals, territorial claims and organised aggression of gang warfare. Sociologists have, in 1985, begun to turn not so much to empirical data on fans but to earlier studies of urban gangs, especially in the USA, as an *entrée* into this increasingly confused story. And evidence came to light during the 1985 season of some spectacular examples of football gangs. Dressed in distinctive (and sometimes expensive) clothes, marshalled by recognised leaders and planned to a precise degree, some of the more recent football gang incidents fit more neatly into older studies of urban gang warfare than they do to the traditional pattern of football support. In this world of gangs, these acts of violence which seem to outsiders as mindless and pointless confer fame and status on the perpetrators. But so too, it has been suggested, does receiving a heavy prison or borstal sentence.[17] And yet, the basic question remains; why football?

In truth the great majority of football fans, those at the games, do not fit the image portrayed here. Those thousands of (primarily male) fans who continue to attend matches, their ranks undoubtably thinning by the season, are peaceable people intent only on watching and enjoying the game; the game, moreover, to which they were, by and large, introduced by fathers, grandfathers, uncles and friends. Football, like other games, has, for more than a century, been bequeathed and inherited across generations of largely urban working men, forming a line of popular cultural descent which has proved one of the most potent, if unnoticed, social features of working-class life. The eruption of hooliganism among certain sections of the fans reflects not so much on the game itself, but on those broader social changes in English urban life, changes which have left exposed key sectors of young adult plebeian life to the unmoderated influences of a certain powerful youth culture, unqualified by older disciplines and unregulated by older, generally sterner hands.[18] The football ground became the place where certain key forms of plebeian youth culture thrived under the curious (and magnifying) gaze of TV cameras – but independent of other peer or elders' pressures which might have provided a modifying antidote. Long before the football authorities or the police were able to intervene, there flourished a self-sustaining culture of fan misbehaviour which drew sustenance from the broader social changes and which blossomed under the glare of publicity and political denunciation. The clubs were at their traditionally unchanging worst; unwilling or unable to act themselves, yet fearful of what might be imposed on them if they failed to act. It was to take a major tragedy to change their position, and only then when bludgeoned by a government which saw in the football malaise the latest in that series of domestic crises which called for action and inspired leadership from Downing Street. If football felt aggrieved at the suggested remedies from the government, they had only themselves to blame for their indecisive ineptitude which trailed back for twenty years and more.

The fans, however, were *not* truly represented by their more violent, vociferous and organised peers. After all, an estimated 15 000 Liverpool fans travelled to Brussels and only a tiny fraction of those were involved in any form of trouble – before, during or after the game. More typical was the English supporter in the long tradition of the travelling football fan; bedecked in club favours, noisy and assertive yet intent on no more than watching a game and expecting to see his team win. But this image of the English fan – no mere caricature but reflective of a long tradition – has been gradually replaced by an altogether nastier image. The problem of English football fans does not recede by claiming that the problem stems from only a small minority. There are legions of examples where marauding minorities have wreaked havoc on a submissive majority. But it is perfectly clear that football – for so long the beneficiary of the improvements in plebeian urban life at certain key junctures in the nineteenth and twentieth centuries – has for the past twenty years been buffeted by many of the harmful deprivations which have disrupted sections of working-class life, deprivations which will be analysed in the second half of this book. By the end of the 1985 season the very people who had been the lifeblood of football – the fans – were openly discussed as the game's most serious debilitating problem. In truth, they – or rather some of them – were only one (albeit the most spectacular) of a series of encircling problems which threatened not only to destroy the game's public esteem, but also to undermine its very existence. Ironically enough in the gradual weakening of football's support, the clubs themselves were extremely important for it was their internal and external weaknesses and ineptitudes which rendered them incapable of coping with their major problems – of which the fans had become the most spectacular.

Part Two
Outside Forces

5   Violence in Context and History

The central problem raised by the Brussels tragedy is that of football violence, or rather violence at and *en route* to and from football matches. To say that it is not new, or that violence is not unique to football is only partly true. Violence among football fans and others has been a feature of crowd behaviour over many centuries, and has caught the attention of recent historians and sociologists. Indeed, the analysis of collective and individual violent behaviour has become a major sub-species of modern sociology, mainly deviance theory, and has both illuminated – and yet sometimes confused – the study of violence. Some of that study amounts to little more than an intellectual conjuring trick, designed to eliminate a modern problem by suggesting, first, that it has existed for a very long time, and secondly by arguing that violence, like other forms of 'deviant' behaviour, is merely a problem of social categorisation, a problem which tells us more about the beholder than the victims or perpetrators.[1] None the less, the modern observer can learn a great deal from such recent studies. We need to place crowd violence in its context; in its long-term historical context and into the broader, more contemporary pattern of violence in modern western societies.

Crowds, almost by definition, posed a threat to the peace and stability of a host of societies in earlier epochs. Before the emergence of modern, urban society (equipped with the mechanical and organisational ability to regulate and control large bodies of people), crowds were regularly the cause and occasion of violence. Often it was accidental violence; an unplanned and unforeseen eruption or spilling over of excitement, panic or sheer pressure of numbers into acts of collective mayhem and killing. Those occasions which attracted large crowds of people – fairs, political meetings, public celebrations, public executions – were frequently marked by turbulence, damage to property, injury and death. Indeed, until the early nineteenth century, English government – in the localities and nationally – was commonly plagued by the problem of crowds and crowd control. Such disturbances were – and remain – highly complex phenomena with a variety of origins: desperation, anger, revenge, the pin-pricks by authority, thoughtlessness or even viciousness by the men in charge – and the entirely fortuitous, contingent and unpredictable trigger mechanisms which can turn a peaceful gathering into a riot.[2] Such factors were as evident in eighteenth-century London as they were in the US cities in the 1960s.[3] In earlier periods, they were legion. In the twenty years between 1790–1810, for example, there were an estimated 740 riots in England, twenty-six of which led to the loss of life. At a later period, between 1834 and 1892 the number of public order offences ran at an annual average of 411 – with much higher 'peaks' at certain times of unrest.[4] Yet it has to be said that the great majority of these incidents were largely 'defensive'; people resisting high prices, enclosures, mechanisation or other difficult problems in a physical manner which has long been familiar to the English historian. The English people had an unenviable reputation throughout western Europe, in the years up to Victoria's reign, as an ungovernable people, long versed in the habits and patterns of popular collective violence.[5]

In the process of urban and industrial change in the nineteenth century, these old English habits were, by and large, reformed and collective violence, in certain crucial areas, gave way to more peaceable and regulated forms of protest and complaint.[6] In part, this was the result of an increasingly effective policing system and a new form of urban and industrial discipline which inculcated the virtues of non-violence and collective restraint among the people of urban England. There were, nevertheless, flurries of violence in late Victorian life and at crucial moments in the twentieth century. During the Boer War, the attacks on Germans and Jews in the First World War, the serious racial attacks of 1919 – these were only the most obvious of a violent collective instinct which, in recent years, has proved all the more shocking because it has become so unusual. It took the major urban disturbances of 1981 (not all of which were 'race riots') to remind us of the possibilities of social unrest of a most violent kind.

This may seem far removed from the particular violence of the Heysel stadium. It is important to stress that the violence in Brussels – however unusual in its deadly results from more traditional forms of urban or football violence – was the culmination of a much longer string of disturbances in and around football matches than many commentators seem to be aware of. It is worth making some basic points about football crowd violence in general before returning specifically to recent incidents. First, football matches have often been the occasion for collective violence. This was particularly true of the pre-modern game which, until the nineteenth century was not only turbulent and ill-disciplined as a game, but also (and for the general reasons already cited) often attracted crowds of boisterous and partisan supporters whose numbers and passions would, and frequently did, lead to crowd disturbances. In the early days of the modern professional teams, violent rivalries – especially between local teams – were not uncommon. In the 1880s, pitch invasions and spectator violence was regular but were effectively brought under control in the 1890s. The most serious problem – and one which often led to trouble – was the size of the crowd and the inadequacy of local organisation and policing.[7] This was spectacularly the case at the opening of Wembley Stadium in 1923 though the outcome was mercifully peaceful. The sheer pressure of people occasionally caused disasters and loss of life. In 1902, for example, part of a new wooden stand at Ibrox collapsed during the Scotland–England match, and 26 people lost their lives and hundreds were injured.[8] Forty years later 33 spectators died and more than 500 were injured at a game in Bolton when the surge of people broke down barriers and spectators were crushed in the ensuing mayhem. Worst of all, and most recent, were the 66 fatalities at the Ibrox match between Celtic and Rangers in January 1971; a result once more of mass panic and overcrowding. Of course, it is reasonable to point out that such disasters were not the direct result of aggression and assaults, but we need to remind ourselves that there has been a miserable tradition of fatalities at football grounds in the past.

The second point to be made is that scenes of appalling crowd violence are not peculiar to Britain (or to games involving British teams and fans). In fact some of the most horrific casualties have occurred far from British influence. In 1964, 318 were killed at an Olympic qualifying game in Peru; in 1968, 72 died in Buenos Aires. Forty-eight lost their lives at a match in Turkey in 1967, 48 in Cairo in 1974. More recently 24 died at a football match in Colombia in 1982, 20 in Moscow in the same year, while a year earlier 19 had died at a game in Greece and 16 in Calcutta. Only a month before the Heysel tragedy, 8 people had been trampled to death at the main stadium in Mexico City.[9] It is perfectly true that, excepting the frightful litany of deaths and injuries, these disasters differed greatly from one another. Some were the direct result of fights among rival fans but most were caused by the capricious forces of overcrowding,

inadequate crowd control, poor facilities and panic among large
numbers of people. It is also perfectly clear that such disasters were,
and are, avoidable; but this was equally true of Brussels.

To suggest that the events in the Heysel stadium were but another
aspect of the long and continuing saga of crowd disturbance would
not be strictly truthful or helpful. What distinguished these events
from others was their immediate, as opposed to their long-term or
fortuitous causes. It was the aggression of one set of fans, in an
inadequately divided section of the stadium, which created panic
among their rivals. Had the organisational and social chemistry
been different – had the arrangements been such that it was Turin
gangs attacking Liverpool fans – it is perfectly conceivable that the
deaths and injuries would have occurred not among Italians but
among the English. This is not, obviously, to excuse what happened
but merely to point out that the events could have had a totally
different outcome. What made that evening less surprising, if no
less sickening, was the well-established reputation of English fans
for their violent behaviour at games in Europe. If many English
people were surprised by the fact that the violence was led by
Liverpool fans (spuriously thought by many in Britain to be devoid
of the violent groups so common to other teams), this was a view not
entirely shared by European fans and observers. A year before,
when that same Liverpool team had travelled to Rome for the
European Cup Final, one local daily proclaimed 'The Barbarians are
Coming'. The referee for that game had the personal protection of a
bevy of karate experts while the stadium itself was ringed by 3000
police. In the event the violence was led by Roman fans (their team
defeated) who rained bottles – and knives – on the visitors.[10]

Whoever the victim or the aggressor in that or other recent acts of
footballing violence, one crucial element in the complex and ghastly
formula is the reputation of English fans. The fact that, by and large,
Liverpool fans were much less troublesome than many other teams
was of no consequence. What mattered was that they were English
fans.

For a decade and more, English teams had afflicted European
cities and stadiums like a pestilence beyond control. If the game of
football had been one of the nation's most abidingly influential
exports, the hooliganism of its fans had become a latter-day curse
which seemed beyond control.

The violent incidents which have plagued British clubs in Europe form a dismal catechism throughout the 1970s and 1980s. The following sample is offered merely to remind the reader of the dossier of fans' misbehaviour accumulating long before the events in Brussels. In 1972, Glasgow Rangers fans rioted in the stadium in Barcelona (taunting the local police with what must have been the incomprehensible cries of 'Fenian bastards'). Three years later, Leeds followers in Paris hurled seating at the CRS. The English national team was followed by similarly marauding gangs which left their distinctive imprint on a host of major cities; Turin, Luxembourg and, in 1985, Helsinki. In the 1983-4 season alone, English fans were involved in violent incidents in Holland and Luxembourg, in Paris, Brussels and Rome.[11] The reputation of the English footballing fraternity went before it. Indeed, so established a phenomenon had it become – both at home and abroad – that it developed its own academic sub-culture, attracting (quite properly) a series of investigations and publications.

It was no surprise that British fans were so disruptive abroad. After all, they had already developed a similar reputation at home when travelling and watching football matches throughout the British Isles. Nor was this merely restricted to the bigger clubs (based in the major cities and therefore, it is so often argued, attracting more than their fair share of local social problems among their supporters). By the early 1980s there was a string of smaller clubs whose following had become infamous for their violence and general misbehaviour. It was to be one of the ironies of the Brussels disaster that Liverpool – and many of the other better supported British clubs – had been less troubled by their fans than many smaller clubs. Primarily this was because the more famous (more successful) clubs had been able to afford the generally costly systems of crowd control and regulation which kept their home crowds rigorously policed and pacified. It was – and remains – generally the case that the bigger, more popular clubs had brought their home crowds under control and were, by and large, able to say the same for their visitors. Clearly, problems remained despite the success of such crowd controls (as Brussels clearly showed) but the problems facing smaller, and generally poorer, clubs seemed to be accentuated by the successes elsewhere.

Again, we must place this problem in its social context, for footballing disturbances were in the short term (as in the long) but one aspect of much broader issue of crowd behaviour. The violence at Brussels, earlier at other European venues and for some fifteen years on British grounds, has been primarily the work of or involving youths and young adults – their ages ranging in the main between 17 and 21 and from working-class origin.[12] It is this age group, or a slightly wider one, which has for a century and more been the object of a great deal of social concern, political disquiet and legal vigilance. It has been customary to isolate that age group between childhood and full manhood (for we are dealing with a masculine issue) as a distinctive 'problem'. Indeed, it was one of the early preoccupations of early psychology as a discipline in the early twentieth century to investigate the particular physical and mental ingredients of the adolescent. The very *concept* of adolescence was itself a function of political and psychological investigation into the behaviour of those boys and young men no longer at school nor yet fully integrated into the no less disciplined world of the work place, or their own family disciplines and restraints.[13] Those forms of rebellious behaviour among adolescents which provoked regular outcries over the past century have normally been described as delinquency, with a consequent effort by the law and the police to control and eliminate them. In essence this was a pathological view of young adults which developed in large part because of the increasing influence of psychology, and which found its most important expression in the development of the British schooling system, most notably through the influence of the psychological work of Cyril Burt.[14] Although much of that theory of human behaviour and development is known to be deeply flawed, this is not at issue. What matters is that for much of the twentieth-century British educational and penal policy towards adolescents has been based on a theory of human development, and entailing a consequent categorisation of age groups, which isolated young adults as a 'problem' group in need of special scrutiny, treatment and, in key areas, punishment.

Over the past generation, however, the intellectual tendency has been to reject this view – to discard the analysis of adolescence as a pathological condition – and instead to seek the explanations for the boisterousness and aggression of adolescents within the context of social class.[15] It is at this point that the sociologists of modern Britain come to our help, and provide us with clues if not with answers to the behaviour of the young. If it is true that the behaviour of these age groups (or rather of some of them) derive from their immediate social and class context (though to phrase it thus seems to state a truism), we need to know what has happened to these working-class communities from whence they spring.

The 'street arabs' of late Victorian life, the adolescents of the early twentieth century, the more ritualised expressions of recent times – of Teds, Rockers, punks and others – all fall into a similar pattern, no matter how different their outward forms and behaviour. All were deeply disliked by outsiders (especially older outsiders), all were viewed, in part if not entirely, as a result of a troubled youthful frame of mind, and all were regarded as threatening forms of behaviour. This is not to say that the behaviour of these particular groups was unexceptional; there is a great deal of evidence to show that each of these youthful sub-cultures (to give them their more recently acquired sociological code) entailed a collective identity which often relied upon violent expression, in word and deed, to impress (especially on outsiders) the strength, the creed and the image of the group identity. If the occasional 'Ted' now seems curiously attractive if only because of his quaintness, it is easy to forget the alarm felt twenty years ago by the violent image of Teddy boys.[16]

It is perfectly natural that any social group perceived as a problem will necessarily become one in the eyes of law enforcement agencies alert to them. The police – and the press – will, understandably, find the very phenomenon they are seeking. But we cannot solve this conundrum merely by claiming this to be a self-fulfilling prophesy, i.e. that without social and legal scrutiny certain forms of anti-social behaviour will simply disappear. In the case of violence – individual or collective – the evidence might, it is true, change quite markedly depending on the zeal or laxity of regulation (and of *recording* the evidence). But this is far from saying that it will disappear if the behaviour which leads to it is not regarded and treated as potentially dangerous or criminal. The boisterousness or violence of certain football crowds will not, after all, disappear if we can reconcile ourselves to ignoring it, or persuading authorities to turn a blind eye to it. It is clear that football fans' behaviour had become progressively worse in the years up to Brussels, in direct relation to the policing systems – and court treatment – designed to contain and punish them. Indeed it is now widely believed that there is a distinct and identifiable deviant known as a 'football hooligan' who is recognisable even to the passing observer. The concept of – and the very term 'a hooligan' – was first adopted by the press in 1898 to

describe unruly urban crowd behaviour.[17] Ninety years later the
term enjoyed a dramatic revival and was directed with great venom
towards sections of football's followers.

Long before the events in Brussels gave this phenomenon a global
audience, football violence had come to be viewed as a special, and a
specially nasty, social problem. It was, furthermore, a problem
which required the closest of scrutiny and the most severe of
punishments. 'Football hooliganism' had, even the late 1970s,
become an extremely emotive issue which prompted demands from
the press and politicians for the sharpest of shocks for convicted
offenders. It is now perfectly clear that this is precisely what they
received. Detailed evidence of the sentencing policies towards
errant football fans shows that in recent years their punishments are
invariably much more severe than those meted out for the same
offences committed at non-footballing occasions. For assaulting or
threatening the police, for using threatening words or behaviour,
for obstruction, for possession of offensive weapons, or for
drunkenness, the football fan is punished more severely than other
offenders. Nor is this merely a matter of courts feeling the offences
to be graver in a crowd; they are, for instance, more lenient even
towards similar offences in political crowds. In fact the very Act
used to punish those arrested in crowd troubles – the 1936 Public
Order Act – although drafted to cope specifically with problems of
political crowds, is now used most severely against football
'hooligans'. Courts have come to see a much greater threat, needing
a much firmer punishment, in recent football rather than political
crowds.[18] This is but one illustration of the central fact which forms
the *rationale* for this book; sections of the football crowd, the 'football
hooligans' have established themselves as a unique and distinctive
social (and political) problem in need of special treatment. And this
was abundantly true long before the early summer of 1985. The
difficulty is knowing when, precisely, the phenomenon emerged.

For all the history of crowd troubles at football matches, the
evidence suggests that between the two World Wars disorderly
behaviour declined at games. Between 1946 and 1960 the number of
recorded incidents ran at about thirteen per season. The figures
doubled in the next six years, and the rituals of violence have
increased year by year thereafter. If Brussels was an accident, there
is a sense in which it was but the appalling culmination of a slowly
developing malaise. There are obviously a number of points which
need to be made here. Perhaps the most important is that the years

when football began to register crowd turbulence in an inescapably noticeable way were the years when mass TV ownership became a prominent feature of English social life. Not only did TV ownership gnaw away at football attendances, but it began to give football intensive coverage. In the years when fewer people attended matches, and ever more people found their main activity watching TV (when about a quarter of all leisure time was spent in front of the television set),[19] television gave ever more coverage to the events on and off the field. What people saw, notably on the terraces, was not merely social reality reflected through the television eye, but forms of crowd activity which drew some of its strength from the presence of television cameras, and which was conveyed to the viewers via the interpretation of commentators, football management and later politicians, who sought increasingly to distance themselves from crowd troubles by bitter denunciation of the trouble-makers. This is, after all, what the newspapers had been doing for years, when describing the Mods and Rockers (in 1964) or the 'hippies' of the late 1960s.[20] For a considerable period a good deal of the popular culture of the young had been consistently reduced to caricature by the media; images of sex, violence and a general social abandon clung to successive generations of young people. But with TV coverage, the added dimension was that many disorders could later be watched by the participants themselves. TV thus held up a mirror, before which groups of young fans could parade their individual or collective actions. Gradually TV was able to single out the football fan as a particular deviant type whose violent behaviour could be seen by everyone with a television set. The resulting public disquiet led the police to look ever more closely at football fans, and to devise new systems for coping with them. This was, it is true, a pattern of events not peculiar to football, but what gave football an added fame was its regularity, its ubiquity and, later, its international nature. Unlike rock concerts, or gatherings of 'Mods' at seaside resorts, football matches were weekly throughout much of the year. Certain groups of young fans were happy to oblige, and to indulge in the very behaviour TV had a natural penchant to project. Footballing misbehaviour consequently spiralled (some obviously planned and orchestrated) with careful police regulation and penal vigour, and an unquenchable TV zest to capture footballing incidents, though it is also true that cameras are sometimes turned away from unpleasant incidents.

There thus developed an international reputation, that English football fans excelled in organised violence (which in many cases was obviously and demonstrably true). Sometimes, however – and perhaps inevitably – the police in Europe, alert to the danger, intervened against English fans even before anything had happened. In the early 1980s, numbers of innocent travelling fans had legitimate grievances against aggressive and in some cases brutal police tactics. This was true at the World Cup games in Spain in 1982. And it was similarly true for numbers of Liverpool fans in Rome in 1984. Yet what happened at Brussels in 1985 was a terrible illustration of the risks of the alternative, of poor or ineffective policing. It takes no great imagination to see that correct (and predictable) policing of the crowd at the Heysel stadium could have averted the disaster. And it is not to feel superior to claim that the accident was unlikely to have happened at a major English ground where policing systems had become extraordinarily adept at containing and controlling football trouble.

Ironically, it has been claimed that this very effectiveness of the policing of major stadiums has been a major factor in shaping the identity and organisation of gangs of football hooligans. To cope with the difficulties, the police and clubs have co-operated to divide and segregate fans into distinct areas and units. There, they are penned in, separated from visitors and detached from more expensive, more respectable fans occupying better facilities. And there, behind their fences, they are ringed by and infiltrated by policemen and, in bigger clubs, scrutinised by police TV cameras. This isolation of groups of younger fans, and their separation from other social or age groups, is the very stuff of their collective identity, though this is also made up of a myriad of very local commitments and passions. Thus the process of controlling crowd disturbances seems likely to have heightened the sense of identity among certain young fans, groups of whom have in the process been transformed into gangs with a territorial claim on their own section of a ground. And into those groups and gangs have been infused the passions – and frustrations – which derive from local communities. Drawn from urban working-class communities beset by mounting social problems, and where deliquent sub-cultures are familiar, such youths have found in their footballing ghettoes a perfect occasion and location for expressing a collective identity. Often, it takes the form of violence, verbal obscenity and racial abuse. Once more, we return to the need to discover more about the changes in English life which have spawned these phenomena.

Although the football grounds have become the occasion and the parade grounds for such violent and collective misbehaviour, the real roots of that behaviour lie elsewhere. On this, most critics of the Brussels disaster are in general agreement, though their explanations are varied and conflicting. We must therefore confront some of the issues which might provide an explanation for this deeply perplexing issue.

6 Racism and Fascism

In the immediate aftermath of Brussels no explanation for what had happened seemed too bizarre to be credible. Those with most to lose – Liverpool Football Club, the local police and the game's organisers – sought to locate the problem beyond their own control, to spread the blame to others. Within hours of the disaster some were pointing to the activities of the National Front, some of whose pamphlets were found in the debris after the game. There were reports of National Front leafleting, of their banners and of their general presence among the fans before the game. Such a presence by elements from fascist groups in English life ought not to have surprised anyone – though much of the reaction to the news took the form of puzzled outrage – if only because for some years English football crowds had been plagued by the attention and presence of the fascists. But this is far from claiming that any National Front presence at Brussels played an instrumental role in the violence which led to the disaster.

In the decade and more before 1985, English football had registered some of the remarkable changes in the politics of the neo-fascist and racist wing in British politics. Equally striking was the increasing numbers of black footballers. In the late 1960s black players were rare, exotic sights on English grounds. A decade ago, they were ubiquitous and had begun to make an impact on the national team. By the early 1980s, there were few major teams without their own black players, and many clubs could boast a number of blacks in their teams. It is now commonplace to see four or five black players in matches throughout all four English divisions. Football was not alone in this, for a host of sports had attracted growing numbers of young blacks. In cricket, boxing, swimming, rugby league, but most of all in athletics, black sportsmen and women came to prominence in the 1970s and 1980s.[1] In a number of areas, black athletes excelled, not only in England but in international meetings, and it became a common sight for the British representatives and winners to be black. This was also true of other nations whose sporting traditions had previously been dominated by white athletes; Canada is a good illustration. And the Canadian pattern had the same origins as the English, for the black sportsmen and women of recent years in both countries came primarily from the West Indian communities which developed in both countries since the 1950s. The offspring of immigrants to Britain have made a remarkable sporting impact in recent years.

By the mid 1970s there were more than half a million people of West Indian backgrounds living in Britain, the great majority of them of working-class origins. Congregated primarily in England's major urban areas, attracted initially to the readily available work in the local industries, West Indians from the first undertook those labouring or dirty jobs others did not want. Like poor immigrants in many societies (including the USA), the West Indians inherited existing social problems, by moving into areas of cheap housing where urban and social facilities were poor and where their lives were beset, increasingly, by the emergence of a malignant racial antipathy which afflicted them at every turn. What made their problems worse was the noticeable onset of British economic decline from the late 1960s. Not only did the offspring of black immigrants begin to face a bleak economic future (unemployment levels among black youths always running dramatically ahead of that among white youths), but they found themselves blamed in certain political circles for the nation's misfortunes.[2]

Young blacks in Britain grew up in communities which were often already influenced by the attachments and loyalties to local football teams. So many of the older stadiums in the urban areas were close to those industrial complexes and their working-class communities which had traditionally given them such loyal support throughout the century. It was then perfectly natural that many young blacks should gravitate towards supporting their local teams in the major cities. It was also predictable that many of these youths would seek in football – and in other athletic activity – the challenges and success which seemed elusive in other walks of life. This had, after all, been a long-established pattern in the USA. There has, however, been a great deal of ill-informed debate about blacks and sporting endeavour. While it is perfectly true that blacks have excelled in a number of sports – in soccer in South America, in athletics and boxing in the USA – their successes are often linked in popular debate with certain 'natural' black abilities. Time and again commentators, notably in the media, are liable to fall back on racial explanations for black athleticism; explanations which impute to black footballers or athletes superior qualities which derive from their racial or ethnic characteristics. The truth of the matter is quite different and it is impossible to understand the black commitment to

certain sports, in Britain or the USA, without coming to terms with
certain seminal social and historical factors.[3]

White society has traditionally tended to write and speak of black
life in flawed, caricatured ways. This is particularly true of black
music which has unquestionably proved extraordinarily influential
on western society. But for many hundreds of years black musicality
– in the slave quarters of the Caribbean and the US south, or more
recently in the Kingston slums or the south side of Chicago – has
been considered a natural, basic human quality in all blacks. It was –
and remains – a popular idea that blacks are in some indefinable way
'naturally' musical. However powerful the hold of music on certain
black communities, it would be hard to deny that what we are
confronting here is a *social* and not a natural, biological
phenomenon. The same is no less true of black athleticism.

Black athleticism – channelled into certain obvious sports – has
been a feature of life in English-speaking societies for many years.
As long ago as the eighteenth century, boxing attracted a number of
prominent black fighters in Britain, notably Tom Molineaux and Bill
Richmond, but it was in the USA that black sportsmen made their
greatest impact. The ending of slavery in 1863 did not fully liberate
blacks in America and it was inevitable that a society deeply
committed to segregation in society at large, informally and more
officially through 'Jim Crow' laws, would also have segregated
sports. Indeed, US sports continued to be racially segregated until
long after 1945, when the dramatic and rapid dismantling of formal
and informal forms of racial discrimination transformed most
aspects of social life in the USA.[4] In the early post-war years black
athletes remained isolated in their own sporting ghettoes, denied
access to the major amateur or professional sporting organisations.
Even the most prominent boxers were white. But the one team
which was allowed access to the white sporting world, the Harlem
Globetrotters, served merely to confirm many of the traditional
white images of black life. They became a vaudeville act; often a
grotesque parody of athleticism, their (often unparalleled) skills
dissolving into pure, ridiculous slap-stick to amuse rather than
excite. They attracted large audiences – black and white – but in the
process confirmed the impression that blacks were skilled, but undisciplined, talented but unamenable to the rigours of team work.
They became, in effect, the clowns of US athleticism – an amusing
diversion when what the players and their black fans needed
was an entrée to the more serious world of competitive sports.[5]

The massive liberating consequences of the Second World War had a profound impact on discrimination in America. Slowly at first, but inevitably too, black athletes began to make an impression and were granted access to the previous white monopolies in the major sports. In football (US), baseball, boxing and athletics, blacks made their impact, especially in the 1950s. But it was really in the 1960s that blacks flooded into US sports. These were, of course, the years when the civil rights movement, voter registration and the efforts of Martin Luther King (and Robert Kennedy) had an important role in galvanising black life in general. In the process there emerged a number of black athletes who personified the urge for black equality. Many of them became the idols of black communities, not merely in America but around the world. Few did more to energise black pride and self-awareness in black achievement than Muhammad Ali (Cassius Clay)[6] – perhaps the greatest boxer of all time. There were, throughout the 1960s and 1970s, serious political and racial problems confronting black sportsmen and women in the USA. But there was no clear line between the broader field of black politics, the massive campaigns for black equality and the elimination of racial discrimination, and the rise of national and well-publicised black sporting prowess. Major sporting events and the more obvious black sporting triumphs served to enhance black claims to equality. The image of the USA was inextricably linked, in the international sporting world, to the efforts and achievements of the major black stars.

The impact of black sporting prowess was felt far beyond America. In Britain, no less than in other more obvious societies (notably in black Africa), the affairs of black America had an important and abiding influence. Two factors conspired to bring this about. First, the revolution in electronics and communications enabled the major events and personalities, from the USA or around the world, to be beamed directly to British homes. Secondly (by the late 1960s), there had developed substantial black communities in the major British cities, communities which though Caribbean rather than American in origin, shared many of the aspirations and frustrations, experienced similar social problems and identified with the style, vocabulary and aims of black life in the USA. In a world where two of the greatest sporting idols were black – Ali and Pele – sport seemed an obvious route to success. Ali himself had admitted, 'I started boxing because I thought this was the fastest way for a black person to make it in this country.'[7] There emerged a

crop of young British black boxers whose obvious model was Ali
(though there were others too), but it was to soccer that many more
black youths turned in the British cities. But in both cases, the
central point to make is that it was the athlete – in a number of
different sports – which became (along with black musicians) the
most significant model and aspiration for generations of young
British blacks denied access to many other areas of conventional
achievement. And this lure of athleticism grew at a compound rate
when a number of local blacks began to make their own distinctive
impact on British sports in the 1970s. In black communities where
successful high achievers were and are in short supply, black
sportsmen seem to be living proof that blacks can indeed rise to
pre-eminence in a white society. Not only that, but black sporting
success often, and obviously, took the form of beating white
competitors. It was scarcely surprising then that the 1970s in Britain
saw the rapid emergence of black sportsmen; in this case an array of
black footballers who aspired to succeed like earlier footballing
blacks, and who saw in the game an obvious route to the fame and
material success denied them and their communities in most other
walks of life.

It is revealing to consider those games where British blacks have
made little headway – in golf and tennis, for instance – to
understand the particular lure of football (or boxing). Football has
traditionally been the game to attract underprivileged young boys
from throughout Britain. Indeed, those areas which continue to
throw up footballing talents disproportionate to their population are
some of the old decaying industrial regions – notably Scotland and
the North-East – where there is a powerful tradition of viewing the
game as the surest and fastest route out of the area.[8] This pattern
seems to have established itself among large numbers of young
blacks; yet there are a number of quirks within the British (and even
US) system which in fact make it *extra* difficult for young blacks to
succeed. Black sportsmen themselves are in general agreement that
they have to be particularly good to be chosen or succeed against
white competition. Equally, black footballers are generally
consigned to subservient roles within a team for, in football as in so
many other areas of British life, the management and officials
subject their black staff to some of the more bizarre and yet
pervasive ideas about blacks and their abilities. Football, like other
sports, is no different from society at large in imputing to its black
participants a number of personal ('racial') qualities, which in fact

reveal more about white attitudes than about black attainments or qualities. Time and again, black sportsmen tell of the basic – and quite open – racial assumptions made of them by their trainers and managers; of the common belief that they lack the 'character' of white team mates or competitors. It seems equally clear that white officials try to get the best performances out of their black players by goading them with racial innuendo and hints. No less influential in persuading black players to strive harder in a game is this racial abuse they receive from their fellow players.[9]

More audible, and perhaps more distressing still, is the racial abuse which has increasingly become an obscene descant at any number of football grounds. The emergence of black footballers in Britain has been paralleled by the development of an ugly racism on the terraces which is used not only to insult black players, but which has spilled over into various and bizarre forms of racism and even neo-fascism. It may seem to some that such concepts – and accusations – are extreme and perhaps unimaginable. Football was, after all (and in some areas still remains), a game which was crucially influential in disseminating the concept of 'fair play'. Yet in England in 1985, not only has overt racism become an inescapable feature of professional football, but fascist extremists have sought to persecute and influence fans at football grounds and to lure them to the more sinister ideas of neo-fascism. Of course, this is *not* to claim that neo-fascist groups have succeeded in their aims. It would be wrong to ignore their influence, their tactics and their impact. We need then to consider why racist and neo-fascist groups should turn to football and its stadiums as a venue for their activities, as a recruiting ground for supporters and for a platform on which to parade their foul ideas.

First, it is important to stress the existence of racism in the game of football. As black footballers became more numerous, so too did the racial abuse, the racial chants and insults spilling from the terraces. Nor was such abuse reserved for visiting players; blacks in the home team were similarly assailed by racist abuse and insults. Again, at one level, this ought not to surprise us if only because England experienced a marked revival of racist and fascist groups in those same years. It is easily understandable why football became the forum for so much racial agitation. It may be true that the game draws its most vocal and persistent support from those young males from inner cities, most afflicted by the dramatic decline in economic and social fortunes and most amenable to the racist suggestions of the National Front and others. But it is equally important to recall that for all their bluster and bombast, racist and fascist political groups have made little effective impact on general elections in Britain. It is obvious and undeniable that in particular localities in a number of major cities, the National Front and related groups have indeed had a malignant impact. As a *parliamentary* force they have remained impotent and even pathetic; an ill-assorted collection of generally peculiar individuals whose most notable achievements have been to secure massive police protection for their provocative behaviour and who have wrapped themselves in the misplaced symbols of national identity, notably the Union Jack. But it would be quite wrong to ignore the appalling physical damage and injuries many of their supporters have inflicted in certain immigrant areas. None the less, neo-fascist groups in England have remained politically marginal to parliamentary politics and have not been able to capture the interest of the national electorate.[10] At football matches, however, they can catch national attention in a way denied them elsewhere.

From the late 1960s, race and immigration have been among the most seminal recruiting agents for that federation of extremist groups which coalesced into the National Front. Time and again, this fascist group blamed black immigration for all the woes and difficulties of contemporary Britain. It is also true that although many of their views about race were echoed by large numbers of the British electorate (the very great majority of whom felt that both major political parties were, at once, too weak and hence directly responsible for black settlement in Britain).[11] Very few people turned in consequence to the National Front. But it is also true that both major political parties progressively adopted immigration policies which were overtly discriminatory. The Front was able to secure a great deal of publicity for its activities, most notably by staging marches into immigrant or sensitive areas, and securing police protection against the inevitable outcry and counter-demonstrations.[12] At football grounds the neo-fascist and racist groups were able to operate more or less unaffected by the traditional restraints placed on their activities. Of course, this is far from claiming that the racist chanting and racial abuse so common at football grounds is solely or even largely a function of organised political groups. Among many of the fans on the terraces, organised into groups or gangs and claiming a 'patch' as their own territory, chanting and choral abuse has become a feature of British football (greatly helped, initially, by the BBC TV's decision to organise a contest for football 'choirs'). This abuse takes a number of forms and is directed against individuals, the visitors, an unpopular manager, even a national figure – and in some particular cases against Jews – and more often against blacks. The pattern also developed of extremist right-wing groups leafleting football grounds, selling their newspapers and displaying their emblems at the games. In this they have been greatly helped by the common use of the Union Jack as a supporters' banner at football grounds. Indeed, the use of the national flag, as a banner, a tee-shirt, another item of clothing, or even as a tatoo or decoration, has been a particular feature of certain groups of English football fans throughout the 1970s and 1980s. The fact that they shared this habit with extreme right-wing groups is in many respects coincidental. But it has served the National Front well by establishing a very visible link and rapport between their own political style and methods of public display and that most commonly adopted by the most ardent and vociferous of young football fans. Clearly, not all Union Jack bedecked fans were supporters of the extreme right; but many were. Moreover, many more could be relied upon, in the security of their own gangs, and safely in their specific territory in the terraces, to join in the racial chanting which flourishes so readily with or without political prompting in the fertile atmosphere of football's terraces.

The problem of analysing the connections between the far right and certain young fans at English grounds is confusing, if only because many of the social and economic forces which have shaped the identity of many younger fans have also served to strengthen the appeal of the National Front. But the causal link between the two remains unclear. In times of marked industrial decline and major urban decay in the areas from which the game of football has traditionally drawn its support, many of the tensions, frustrations and antipathies of local life are likely to find expression in local football, though this is equally true of other forms of contemporary popular culture. There remains, however, a number of contemporary and historical conundrums. Why does racism (and violence) plague professional football and yet, so far, make negligible impact on other neighbouring sports? Leeds United has become infamous for the violence and racism of its fans. But Leeds rugby league club continues to provide family entertainment.[13] Similarly, if the problems besetting the modern game are related to the economic decline of the country and particularly to the scourge of unemployment, why was this not the case fifty years ago when similar regions were no less afflicted by massive deprivation? Such questions are easily posed, much less easily answered.

To claim that football has merely come to reflect the uglier side of modern English racism – which may be true in fact – does not provide an explanation of why this has happened. But it is quite extraordinary that in the aftermath of Brussels many observers should have noted, effectively for the first time, the presence among English fans of extremist political groups. Football crowds have throughout the 1970s been a fertile soil for some of the nastier features of English urban life, of which the malignancy of collective and well-publicised racism is perhaps one of the most dangerous. It is one of those extraordinary ironies that, in years when black sportsmen (and women) have begun to make a major impact on English life, they do so, in certain sports, to a mounting descant of racial abuse. It was customary for observers of US sports to see the rise of local black athleticism as evidence of the disintegration of racial barriers and antipathies. 'Negroes approach closer to the democratic ideal in the world of sport than in any other facet of American life'; 'the participation of the Negro in sport has been a significant development in bringing him into the mainstream of American life'.[14] We know that such views seem, in many respects, particularly naive and optimistic. Less promising still perhaps is what has happened in contemporary England. The national game was singled out in the 1985 report of the Commission for Racial Equality for the commonplace racism among its fans. Indeed, the behaviour of those fans was presented as evidence for the *worsening* of racial attitudes and relations in contemporary Britain.[15] Thus, in the summer of 1985 the national game was encircled by a rising chorus of official, governmental, legal and international public abuse. The criticisms of the professional game of football were *not* inspired uniquely by the events in Brussels. Even had that disaster *not* taken place, there was an abundance of concerns facing football – and English society at large. The impact of racism at football grounds was sufficient to alarm the Commission for Racial Equality, charged with scrutinising racial matters. Football was seen as the occasion, and possibly the cause, of a number of major contemporary problems, even before the Brussels affair subsumed all other related matters into one horrible and yet apparently inexplicable act of collective violence and death. If extreme right-wing groups *had* been present at the Brussels game this alone would be quite unexceptional, if only because they were commonly to be found at English matches. It would, however, be quite extraordinary if the events at that match had been *caused* primarily by their presence; or, even more incredibly, by their literature. To suggest that the disaster was, in some inexplicable way, the work of a fascist fringe requires us to suspend credibility and to set aside what we know about the immediate and long-term causes of crowd violence. Yet it still remains a deeply disturbing fact that English football fans now regularly display a degree of overt and collective racism of a kind normally reserved for the demonstrations and meetings of the wilder fringes of right-wing politics.

There is, quite clearly, a degree of 'basic' racism among these fans. As we have seen before, it would be unusual if a society in which racism was a basic (if generally dormant) feature of life did not send eddies of that racial tension into the participation, management, playing and spectating of major sports. Football, at this level, merely acts as a seismic recorder for deeper social turbulence. But this obviously is far from a satisfactory answer. Could it be that we need to return to the formative presence of the media, notably television, at football grounds? In the summer of 1984 a black player in the English team playing in Chile was booed by English fans who had travelled thousands of miles apparently to wave their right-wing political favours and abuse black players. They knew, of course, that their actions would be promptly picked up by TV cameras and newspaper photographers. A political organisation which could never expect more than a minimal coverage by the media at home – and a mere handful of electoral votes at national elections – had secured massive, albeit notorious, coverage by the simple tactic of racial abuse; a tactic employed every Saturday in the football season. That incident alone provides an important clue; that fascist and racist political groups use the facilities of the football ground not only to recruit and to disseminate their ideas (in which they may well be unsuccessful), but more importantly they use the stadiums as a platform from which they can project their venomous views, in the simplest and most offensive of forms, into millions of homes. It is, at once, both obvious and yet important that the racism of the far right can achieve greater (and cheaper) publicity at a major football match than they can hope to achieve by years of conventional political campaigning. TV coverage provides an instant and easy route into the nation's homes, though this does not mean that the viewer will be persuaded accordingly. It is hard to deny that football has come to be afflicted by the expanding and seemingly uncontrollable malignancy of racism. Moreover, this was abundantly clear – indeed it was audible – long before Brussels focused attention on the violence of English fans.

7 The Distorting Mirror: The Media and the Game

What made the tragedies at Brussels and Bradford doubly shocking was the fact that they were transmitted live to millions of homes by television. Clearly, the events which took place would have been no less horrifying had they not been acted out in front of TV cameras, but it was the fact that millions of people, keen only to watch a game of football, found themselves unwittingly *voyeurs* to a grizzly tragedy which added an extra dimension to the reactions to those events. True, the TV cameras were, initially, as innocent as any casual observer, caught up in a mounting tragedy which they had not expected or wanted. But they became, instantly, an instrumental agent in the way the tragedy came to be perceived by millions of people. TV became, not for the first time, a prism which refracted social reality into the homes of the British people. It could be countered that television is merely a passive instrument; an inert mirror which merely reflects events into the nation's front room. But too much evidence is now available for anyone to accept such claims unquestionably. There is in fact an academic growth industry – centred primarily on the Media Group at Glasgow – which has amply illustrated the way in which TV is far from being a passive agency in the dissemination of information and news.[1] Few who watched the events unfold at the Heysel stadium could be left in any doubt of the case; as the films were replayed, frozen, magnified – and all to the accompaniment of commentary which became, at times, a descant of abuse and straightforward silliness. Much was said, in the heat of the moment, which was regrettable but forgivable. Much more of what was said was revealing of a deeper antagonism towards a number of major changes in recent English history. Yet few of the commentators involved seemed aware of their own role in the night's events.

Even a cursory glance at the history of TV – and the media at large – would have revealed a persistent and influential effect upon the nation's perceptions of the world around them and of its major problems. Football now seemed to be in a crisis because the violence

which attended it was a regular and inescapable event on the
television. We need, therefore, to consider more fully the way in
which the crescendo of football violence was portrayed to people
through the TV eye.

The development and success of modern football – and of a wide
range of sport – has been inextricably bound up with the coverage
received in the media for a century past. In fact football's rise to
popularity a century ago was closely linked to the development of a
highly literate society which came to depend for information upon
the printed word, later the radio and more recently television.
Newspapers, magazines and boys comics were active at an early
stage in promoting and exploiting the manifest interest among
males in football. Nor was this merely a question of factual
reporting, for the press – involved in a commercial battle for the
readership of working men – was instrumental in elevating
footballers into 'stars' and in encouraging local commitments and
loyalties to particular teams.[2] Compared to more recent
developments, the press coverage of football before, say 1914,
seemed both tame and moderate. But in essence it bears all the
ingredients to be found in the relationship between the media and
the game today. Football 'specials' with the day's results,
newspaper articles by and about teams and players, commenting on
and criticism of the conduct of the clubs and teams – all this was
commonplace long before the coming of the television cameras. The
process was transformed in between the wars by mass radio
ownership. In common with a host of other forms of entertainment
(and instruction) the radio 'domesticated' much of the nation's
leisure pursuits by enabling millions of people to seek their pleasure
at home.[3] Initially this may have been of greater importance for
women (notably working-class women) rather than men who had
traditionally enjoyed a number of entertainments away from home.
Similarly the mass ownership of a radio seems to have reinforced
rather than replaced certain leisure pursuits. Football was reported
and the day's results presented on the radio long before the decline
in attendance became noticeable. But the radio was the harbinger of
things to come; of the redirecting of a great deal of mass
entertainment away from the public place – be it the music hall,
cinema or football stadium – and into the home.

At first, sport in general was slow in securing a major role in TV
coverage; initially the pattern was largely that already established by
the newspapers and their treatment of sport. The BBC led the way in

TV sports coverage. The independent commercial companies were, to begin with (in the mid 1950s), not very interested, primarily because their advertisers devoted their commercial attentions to female viewers who were not, by and large, thought to be interested in sports. All this began to change after 1960, and even more quickly after the introduction of colour TV. Television companies of all sorts and conditions began to specialise in sports coverage, equipping themselves with specially trained staff and equipment. And the sports, in their turn, began to transform themselves into TV sports; or rather into games in which their most important and most lucrative aspects were geared towards TV. Sporting moments, achievements, skills – and stars – could be captured in stunning detail, in slow motion, in frame-by-frame replay on the TV screen. And tens of millions – sometimes hundreds of millions – of people could be guaranteed to watch and to share the instant entertainment in the comfort of their own homes. Sports rapidly became even more commercial than ever before; some sports emerged from a well-deserved obscurity into national and then international fame, thanks to the presence of the TV cameras and the commercial value it was able to attach to the sports it covered. Two sports which had been local and non-commercial (darts and snooker) had by 1980, and solely thanks to TV, become remarkably popular. By 1980 snooker was second only to soccer in its popularity among British men. Moreover, the popular press, struggling for survival in the 1970s and locked into a fierce battle, with the tabloids, quickly emulated television, devoting ever more space to sports, and inflating sporting personalities into star positions (not merely on the sporting pages).[4]

The impact of TV has served to make television sports – of which soccer is but one – even more commercial – and lucrative – for some of its major figures. While only a minority of soccer players are able to capitalise substantially on this commercial fame, those involved are able to enjoy the trappings of material wealth which an earlier generation of sportsmen could scarcely have dreamed about. Thus the commercial stakes are extraordinarily high, with the consequent infusion into the game of an element of commitment and passion which seems sharper than in earlier epochs. There is, commercially, much more at stake. Footballers – like snooker or tennis players – stand to lose more than a game in defeat, a fact which may well be partly responsible for the apparent changes in sporting behaviour among the players.

It is abundantly clear then that TV has utterly transformed the nature and course of those games and sports it has projected into people's homes. But it has also changed the role – and the behaviour – of spectators in a number (but not all) of those games. It is a simple matter to suggest that the transformation in crowd behaviour started to make itself felt at the time TV began to cover games. But it is much more difficult to establish a *causal* link. There is evidence that the presence of cameras does in certain crucial ways affect the behaviour of players, no less than crowds. The gesticulations which follow success or failure are often directed not at the spectators but at the cameras perched around the ground. Similarly, spectators can often be seen carrying banners and placards which are directed not at their opponents at the stadium but at their invisible opponents – or admirers – watching on TV. The Brussels game proved the point perfectly. There were a number of Liverpool flags and banners directed against Manchester United and their fans, a fact which must have puzzled their Italian opponents or their Belgian hosts. But at this level the influence of TV is obvious and undeniable; it is merely holding up a mirror in front of which the more narcissistic players and fans besport themselves, generally innocently but sometimes with more sinister ambitions. Much more difficult is to assess the relationship between the TV presence and violence, individual or collective.

In a sense the TV camera ought to deter violence. Frozen frames of action can easily identify and isolate offenders (both on and off the field), a fact often used in disciplinary hearings and, in the aftermath of Brussels, in trying to locate ringleaders of the Brussels violence. It may be one of the more sinister developments in recent years that some of those active in crowd violence have begun to cover their faces, with scarfs or balaclavas – as many do in violent political demonstrations – to prevent identification. But this is, again, merely to note the obvious. More subtle and therefore more difficult to assess is that culture of violence, which is so basic to TV, so huge a part of TV's daily offerings and so endemic to its entertainment. Violent football fans may have become an element, albeit real rather than fictional, in the continuing saga of TV violence. This is, of course, a basic and persistent complaint from a wide range of viewers' organisations, led most notably by Mrs Mary Whitehouse. But it is not necessary to share her political and social outlook to accept the fundamental point, which is confirmed time and again in a host of surveys, that violence forms a major part in the output of most TV companies. Indeed this point is *so* obvious that it has become unnoticeable; so integral to TV entertainment that most viewers fail to notice the problem. There are times when fictional violence and social reality can be confused; the violence of films or plays is so realistically portrayed as to blur the distinction between fact and fiction. This process similarly blurs the reactions of the viewer who often fails to see any distinction between fiction and reality.

Over the past generation, the technological advances has enabled television instantly to project violence, often of the most appalling kind, into the home. Riots, brutal killings, air crashes, major fires, road accidents, terrorist bombings, the Vietnam War – all these and more are portrayed in the finest and most graphic detail. Sights which were once happily preserved for the staff of the emergency services are now seen regularly by millions of people in their homes. The disasters at Bradford and Brussels fall into that category, for the presence of television cameras enabled millions of people to watch as innocent victims were incinerated or crushed. Two questions immediately spring to mind when considering the violence of football crowds. First, does the existence of a broader culture of violence, notably that projected on TV, provide a key element in the complex chemistry of crowd behaviour (but if it does, why does it do so in some sports and not in others)? Secondly, does the presence of TV cameras itself act as a stimulant to those young men (often organised into gangs); does TV become the stage upon which the petty and often base-minded antipathies of certain groups can be transformed into a *bravura* of collective violence? Not surprisingly perhaps the answers to these and other questions are often dependent on a person's broader political and social outlook. We need to see if there is any objective evidence which might help us cut a path through the inevitable confusion.

Violence – of all sorts – has been a major element in popular culture since the development of modern mass literacy in the late eighteenth century. Broadsheets, woodcuts and ballards recounting the ghastly details of murders and violence were the precursors of the more popular national newspapers of the nineteenth century. Travelling shows, fairgrounds and popular theatre normally portrayed violence to a degree which incurred the wrath of contemporary propertied society. In 1851, *The Edinburgh Review* thought that the popular theatre was

a powerful agent for depraving the boyish classes of our towns
and cities . . . the boy who is led on to haunt them becomes
rapidly demoralised, and seeks to be the doer of the injuries that
have interested him as a spectator.[5]

But all this was qualitatively different from the visual attention paid
to death and suffering, almost daily, on television screens over the
past generation.[6] Although it may be true that the portrayal of the
great bulk of violent criminal activity on TV is thought to be from the
police viewpoint – or at least from a position critical of the criminals[7]
– this does not deflect the central assertion of the pre-eminent role
assigned to crime and violence on TV. But the social influence of that
violence continues to bemuse investigators. Moreover, there are
legions of professional researchers currently scrutinising the
relationship between TV violence and society; in universities,
government departments and within television companies
themselves. And this is more especially the case in the USA. But the
accumulation of evidence does not lead to agreement among those
researchers, for there have been conflicting interpretations of the
data available. None the less, those arguments which have sought
to illustrate the causal links between TV and social violence have
been seized upon by pressure groups and politicians keen to bridle
and license the output of what they regard as socially unhealthy TV.
For their arguments, the events in Brussels provided, or so it
seemed, confirmation of all they had claimed for years past; that
television violence begets social violence – though now on a
horrifying scale. Yet recent research among viewers suggests that
fictional violence on TV elicits paradoxical responses among the
viewers; there is, for instance, an extraordinary variation in what
viewers even regard or perceive as violence. Research sponsored by
the IBA has illustrated that

> fictional violence cannot be defined in simple terms as a single
> unitary entity. Violence is a complex feature of fictional
> programming and viewers' sensitivities to it may be highly
> discriminating.[8]

At the heart of much of the criticism of violence on TV is the
assumption that it has proved inordinately influential among the
young. Again, there is an abundance of data to show that millions of
children and young adults watch huge quantities of TV each day[9]

(often at times designated by television companies for more 'adult' viewing). It is often assumed that the exposure of the young to such hours of viewing (often regarded as excessive), in conjunction with the violent nature of much of the content of TV (from cartoons through to news coverage), serves to encourage a tolerance and even a liking for violence. Whether true or false, the link has been made between the particular problems of childhood and adolescence, and the influence of TV.[10] Again, we need to remind ourselves that for the best part of a century, childhood and adolescence have been singled out as distinct 'problem' areas of behaviour and personal development, primarily because of the pervasive influence of psychology. To suggest that the incomprehensible behaviour of groups of 'teenagers' or young men at football grounds often falls into this pattern is not to claim that the 'problem' is merely a reprise of a traditional pattern. But the fact that football violence has tended overwhelmingly to be a young phenomenon has helped to reinforce the commonplace assumption that certain sections of the nation's young are being ill-served by the excessive exposure they receive to TV violence.

Football's violent offenders – young, ill-educated, low status and income – seem to offer a perfect sample to illustrate the point. Yet it requires no training in psychology or social surveys to see that they may indeed by utterly untypical of a more general phenomenon. It may well be that the link between violent behaviour (at football grounds) and the violence of TV is much more confused than is often imagined. The violent behaviour may be more a result of conditions other than the exposure to violent television – a possibility argued by social psychologists who have experimented on the relationship between violent behaviour and TV violence.[11] It is in many respects extremely difficult to isolate the influence of one particular variable – in this case the TV viewing – from a complex social web of determinants which shape an individual's social behaviour. In fact there is contrary evidence which suggests that these young boys/men whose leisure time – and style – is shaped on the streets, spend (obviously) less time in the home and therefore receive relatively *less* exposure to TV than their peers from better-off homes where leisure life is much more home-based (and therefore TV-dominated).[12] The thrust of this basic point is to lead us to a subject which in many respects remains oddly ignored – the family.

We know from the recent interest in certain forms of violence – child abuse, wife-battering and sexual assault – that the family is the crucible from which there emerges a host of personal and social problems.[13] Yet many sociologists who have sought to locate the problems of violence (among football fans and others) have generally turned their back on this, the most formative social organisation in modern British life. Moreover, even if we are interested solely in the impact of television on childhood and adolescent development, it is often forgotten that television viewing is largely determined and qualified by the family and its domestic condition. The tolerance of, or opposition to, watching television, the restrictions of viewing hours or the nature of programmes allowed – all these and more are obviously a function of domestic and family conditions. Thus it is probable that much of the influence of TV is mediated, filtered, through the particular family; with its own values, and disciplines – or lack of them. Clearly this is far from claiming that everything depends on the family. But it seems likely that the family will be as important an ingredient in a growing child's perception of the outside world (in this case, seen via television) as the television programmes themselves. At one level this may seem so obvious as to be unremarkable. But it is also true that a great deal of the literature which has addressed itself to the problems of social violence (especially as an element in modern youth culture) has ignored the role of family life.[14]

Contrary to the feeling that TV violence begets social violence, there is evidence to suggest that it is likely to encourage people to seek and expect stronger authority and sterner action by the agencies of law and order. In addition, TV violence may be less significant in *stimulating* acts of violence than it is in encouraging a stiffening of the law and order lobby. In this sense the revulsion felt by many at the violence they witness on television is part of a longer tradition, substantially generated by the media, of 'panic' at the breakdown of law and order. The particular issues which reveal this panic differ from one period to another – 'mods and rockers' in the 1960s, 'mugging' in the 1970s and more recently an epidemic of soccer violence.[15] Yet one can readily recognise the role of the media, the press and TV, in inflating and proclaiming such outbursts. But it would be quite absurd to suggest that the more outrageous outbursts of such behaviour – in this case soccer violence – were merely or even largely a function of media manipulation. However true it may be that the Brussels disaster led to a series of draconian measures, in Britain and abroad, this was a direct consequence of scenes of quite extraordinary violence and destruction, and not merely a media campaign of distortion.

There remains at the heart of social violence (in this case football violence) an element of irrationality which cannot be ignored, or dispensed with, by merely imputing to those involved values and attitudes which suit the researcher's thesis. Of course, it could be argued that irrationality is itself an important social quality. But what still has to be explained is why the outbursts of violence, culminating in Brussels, are more pronounced, more intense and more uncontrollable at football grounds? It is at this point that television as a causal factor in football violence begins to appear less convincing. If violence erupts in front of the camera, why not at rugby, or even tennis matches? Clearly there is something distinctive about the soccer crowd – or some of them – which has rendered them into a volatile and dangerous substance. Yet if this were due to television alone (or even primarily) it would be reasonable to expect disorders wherever the cameras were to be found. It is not improbable that the ingredients for social violence may be present in a number of crowds but that the spark which ignites a disturbance is accidental and quite unpredictable. At Brussels the crucial spark was not so much the composition of the crowd, but the precise order and manner in which they were assembled, marshalled and controlled. Once the violence began, however, it became a spectacle which TV cameras could not resist.

It is not an act of cynicism to feel that the sights of the disaster, the subsequent battles between fans and the police and the protracted pacification of the stadium proved a better spectacle than the match itself. After such scenes of almost Roman carnivale, football was a mere afterthought; a game whose false aggression and artificial combats could scarcely compare with the real life and death battles of the preceding two hours. This is a point more than amplified by the fact that countries which were not destined to broadcast the game were none the less happy to concentrate on the ghastly details of death and suffering. Once more, television proved its importance in capturing the awfulness of human tragedy.

There is a shocking symmetry to the argument. The agency which has proved influential beyond all imagination in entertaining millions of people – TV – is now on hand to transform human suffering into a form of popular entertainment. This is almost a return to the pre-industrial world where the carnivals and executions were among the most popular forms of entertainment. That it is able to do so is a function not merely of technology, but of its tradition in making palatable and entertaining, violence of all sorts and conditions. Of course, it might be argued that the curiosity about and desire for violence is, like the urge for food or sexual satisfaction, a basic human response.[16] While it may be difficult to prove the causal influence of TV violence, it is undeniable that acts of violence, purveyed on television, have become a major theme in television coverage. Nor is this simply a matter of fictional entertainment for there have been any number of major violent phenomena which have been witnessed by millions on TV. The degree to which this – part of a long and cumulative process – has had the effect of desensitising the viewers to acts of violence is difficult to assess. Again, the evidence is contradictory and confusing. In the Falklands War, the government took elaborate precautions to prevent the scenes of wartime death and pain and of maimed survivors reaching the British public, in order to avoid the sort of outrage felt at home by US television coverage of American sufferings in Vietnam. Clearly, the public, on both sides of the Atlantic, has not been desensitised to the point of insensibility in matters of domestic or patriotic affairs. Indeed, this may provide a clue to the outrage felt at the Brussels disaster. Here, after all, was an international venue, a clash between two nations which, though sporting in form, inevitably took on the appearance of a clash between two nations. Yet it was, after all, only a game. What happened, though, was much more than a game. In a sport which had pioneered the concept of gentlemanly behaviour, the violence of the crowd was a denial of all that the game had been devised to project and embody. Television, instead of projecting the best of sporting values, revealed to the world some of the nation's worst social problems. These problems had, it is true, long been familiar up and down the country and, periodically, in Europe, although on this occasion the full ugliness of English social violence was beamed around the world. Ultimately it may have had little to do with football itself. But, via that most potent image-maker, television, the English game of football portrayed to millions of people around the world an image of national life which, however skewed, unrepresentative and distorted, none the less embodied a new social reality about England in the mid-1980s.

8   Codes of Discipline

The search for an explanation of the Brussels tragedy took critics into a broad criticism of most of England's contemporary institutions – few of them offering an easier target than the state of the nation's schools. Of course, it needs to be stressed that any analysis of the behaviour of fans in Brussels which turns to the school system must inevitably concentrate on Liverpool's schools – or rather on the schools of those men known to have been involved in the troubles. What happened, however, was an attempt to explain the particular (the Brussels disaster) by reference to the general (the 'decline' in the school system). It is abundantly clear that the major economic decline of Liverpool itself had been reflected (perhaps inevitably so) in serious social and educational problems within the city's schools.[1] But for many, this was merely part of a *national* problem. In the words of Richard West, 'The collapse of teaching and discipline in our schools . . . is nowhere more evident than in Liverpool.'[2] In that official weekly guide of the teaching profession, *The Times Education Supplement*, two authors remarked:

> In the furore about football hooliganism, it should not be overlooked that, just like every madman, psychopath and delinquent, they have spent something like 15,000 hours in the classroom – less, of course, any all-too-likely truancy.[3]

The flippant answer to such a general point is that since *everyone* undergoes this experience, how can it explain the behaviour of a small minority – of hooligans or psychopaths? There is, once more, an abundance of evidence which might provide some answers.

Research into the behaviour of pupils in schools – in Europe as well as England – suggests that teachers and heads are convinced that the problem of disruptive pupils is increasing. In many schools, 'the price of peace' is the acceptance by teachers of the simple refusal of many pupils to conform and to learn. Difficult classes abound, especially in the inner cities, and even experienced staff are flummoxed by their inability to cope with some of the difficult schools created by reorganisation.

It is clear that schools are in many respects merely reflecting much broader social problems – that they are as much the victims as the perpetrators of social problems. To put the matter boldly – but not unrealistically – in an urban community with generally low income, high unemployment, poor housing conditions, a high incidence of marital discord and single-parent families, high local levels of crime and few consequent community or familial restraints on the behaviour of children, the local schools can hardly hope to instil a discipline lacking elsewhere. To isolate the schools from this complex social fabric – to suggest that they alone must bear the sole or dominant responsibility for the behaviour of their pupils or ex-pupils – is to misunderstand the role, the limitations and the potential of schools in any community. The criticism directed at the schools, locally or generally, is to miss the point that large numbers of children and young people in England have become the victims of a quite dramatic and complex series of changes in socialisation. The tight codes of discipline, overlapping and mutually reinforcing, in traditional working-class communities – within the family, the school and then the work place – have all been progressively changed or partly destroyed by the economic and social forces which have transformed and largely disfigured the face of urban England. This is far from claiming that all was well in earlier generations; that what we have lost is a warm, close-knit Hoggart-like series of plebeian communities which successively instilled an unquestioned sense of personal discipline and collective identity. But it is unquestionably true that what has emerged throughout urban England in the past generation is a series of interrelated structural (and partly political) changes which have created profound and, as yet, incalculable changes in personal and collective behaviour. For reasons which need to be explained these changes seem to have found their most dramatic outlet and release among small groups of young people at football grounds.

The communities which have been the traditional foundation for support for soccer have been transformed, most spectacularly by urban renewal and rehousing. Although it is true that hundreds of thousands of old, and largely inadequate, traditional houses remain, the 1950s and 1960s were characterised by the destruction of older working-class communities and the redirection of population into new estates and especially into high-rise blocks. Many rapidly became problem areas where vandalism and violence were commonplace, but though the problems (and the mistakes) were readily recognised, the money was no longer available, by the mid-1970s, to rectify the errors of earlier years.[4] The consequence was that a new generation of young people were being born into deprived urban circumstances which, if quite different from the bleakness of pre- and immediately post-war working-class life, were quite devoid of many of the familial and social restraints which had been characteristic of earlier working-class life. The architectural violation of English cities is too obvious to need repetition, though again we need not romanticise the meanness of earlier working-class housing. But it does need to be stressed that the rehousing of millions of urban working people was, at heart, a social experiment which went disastrously wrong.

The motives behind this urban revolution were mixed. There was the sheer greed (and corruption) of the building industry and its political clients, but there was, by the same token, an unshakable optimism that what was being created was a new Jerusalem for people long accustomed to being the victims of a more heartless urban and industrial environment. Left-wing politicians and critics lauded the opening of new estates and tower blocks as the final break with communities created in the infamous period of harsh industrial expansion of the nineteenth century. The brutalism of the new developments were manifest from the first; by the time it became clear that they had endemic physical and social problems, the national economy had entered a new and altogether more depressing phase. The result was that in all of England's (and Scotland's) major cities a new generation of working people – though now without the work – were left marooned on their estates and in their towers, bereft of local, community or wider family support and ties (so basic to older urban communities) and enduring bleak material conditions which often defied belief.[5] It was from this bleak urban environment that new generations of deprived English children entered a school system which was itself utterly transformed in the same years.

Compulsory schooling has been a major feature of English life for more than a century and it is important to recognise that its role throughout that period was, by intent and exercise, as much social as it was purely educational. After 1870 the gathering together of all the nation's children under the school roof was a powerful force not merely in encouraging literacy and learning, but in inculcating a number of important social qualities which were of prime importance to the smooth conduct and development of social and economic life after schooling. In the years before the coming of compulsory schooling, Victorian cities were keen to see its introduction in order to remove the vast armies of children from the streets of urban England and to instil in these apparently undisciplined hoards of urchins the disciplines and social virtues they appeared to be lacking.[6] Schooling for plebeian boys and girls was viewed not as a means of providing greater social opportunities in adult life, but in cementing a commitment to the social class and sex roles to which nature and circumstance had destined them. Compulsory education became – what it was intended to be – a major agency in the more complete socialisation of successive generations of working people in an advanced industrial and urban society. Children went to school because they were obliged to do so and although their attitude was often one of truculence, resistance and an unwillingness to learn, the end result was a process of socialisation which involved important disciplines; the disciplines of the clock, obeying the instructions of superiors. Schools produced a varied disciplinary diet involving appearance, tidiness and general obedience, all of which were of key importance in adult life.[7]

Schooling inevitably changed greatly in the course of the twentieth century, most notably the development of the selected, tripartite system of the Act of 1944. But the post-war results of that Act seemed to many critics to have reinforced the unhealthy social, class divides in society at large. Working-class children seemed to be consistently discriminated against while their social superiors took the lion's share of places in better schools and in higher education. The Labour Party, anxious to reverse this trend, actively promoted comprehensive schools, abolishing grammar and direct schools and pressurising independent schools (normally through empty threats). By the late 1970s the overwhelming majority of the nation's pupils were in comprehensive schools, substantial numbers of which were purpose-built and close to the new urban developments of the 1960s. Of more than 11 million pupils in English schools by 1977, only 614 000 were in private or assisted schools.[8] Paradoxically, private education flourished because though more costly they offered facilities which many parents found lacking in the state system. Yet the comprehensive system was itself uneven in facilities and achievements. Not surprisingly comprehensives in more well-to-do areas had superior educational records to schools in poorer, more deprived communities. It had become abundantly clear by the late 1970s that for armies of children, notably from poor inner city areas, the move to comprehensive schooling had not achieved the educational and social ideals expected by the politicians responsible for the educational changes.

There was in fact a close and quite distressing symmetry of problems, for the failure of the urban renewal schemes and the often appalling housing conditions to be found in the new developments paralleled the failures and frustrated ambitions in education. Once more, the victims of social deprivation found themselves assailed on all sides. Deprived of the material and social benefits of their traditional communities, and finding themselves instead incarcerated in friendless developments, large numbers of poor working people now found their children obliged to endure the worst (and worsening) educational facilities in the country. To make matters worse, the future prospects for those people were worse than for any group of working people since the Second World War; after a more than inadequate education, the main prospect of early adult life was that of joining the queues of the unemployed.

It was (and is) in the poor comprehensive schools in deprived inner city areas – the heartland of traditional, but now fragmented, dispersed and dislocated, working-class life – that teachers were happy merely to maintain peace. To come to a mutually acceptable tolerance was as much as many hard-pressed teachers could hope to achieve; any ambition of providing a lively or useful education was relegated to the prime need simply to keep the peace. Thus for many pupils in the more difficult schools, education became a meaningless routine – with the inevitable consequences for the pupils' attainments by the end of schooldays (despite raising the leaving age to 16). More alarming too, for society at large, was the fact that many schools were unable to socialise large numbers of their pupils to the disciplines and rigours which had been basic to compulsory schooling for a century. Of course, we need not accept in its entirety the idealised view of the highly disciplined and effective training of schooling in earlier generations. There is, after all, a wealth of information which illustrates the failures and shortcomings of schooling among working-class pupils over the past hundred years. None the less observers of the English education system have been united in seeing a developing crisis in many schools in the major urban areas. And that crisis is only in part about teachers' pay and educational standards. Central to the problem is the schools' ability – or inability – to inculcate a collective and responsible discipline among large numbers of pupils who live in communities marked by changes in familial or community disciplines. It is unreasonable to expect schools to make good the social failings of the communities they serve. Schoolteachers, however talented, energetic and committed, cannot hope to compensate for the family difficulties, poor housing, low income (or unemployment) and poor health conditions which shape the immediate environment of many of their pupils. Now – as at any period we care to examine in the past century – the schools reflect the problems and difficulties of their host communities; to expect them to counterbalance those problems, to provide an antidote to social ailments, and to provide a useful education (all at a time of material and financial crisis in schools) is to expect the impossible.

The simple truth is that many schools have become a platform on which are paraded a host of interrelated social problems; the schools are the occasion and not the cause of those ills. Yet the schools are also political instruments – institutions in the hands of local and national politicians. And it is irresistibly tempting for many politicians to blame schools for any of the social ills which are manifested among the young or young adults. But those same schools – and the broader educational system – have in a marked degree been given shape, direction and purpose by those politicians. How many politicians responsible for the changes in education (or housing) since the 1960s are prepared to accept public responsibility for those institutions' shortcomings? When they do, it is rarely with the alacrity they claim credit and honours for their attainments. Once more, we are faced with a familiar pattern – of buck-passing. It is all too easy to blame teachers and schools for the various problems and shortcomings to be found among their pupils and ex-pupils. Thus it was that schools – and schoolteachers – were an obvious target for some critics of the Brussels disaster and of soccer violence in general. In the aftermath of the disaster, one popular newspaper thought that schools were 'turning out an army of disaffected youths, illiterate and loutish. They are true lumpen proletariat – disinherited and disfranchised by their own ig-norance'. This was a view which was pushed to its logical and most offensive extreme by Auberon Waugh, in his now familiar role of basher of working people:

It is the behaviour of the classroom which has now, in a magnified form, invaded the football terraces. The real villain, I fear, is a streak of wetness which runs through the entire administrative class in Britain.

Waugh's subtle solution was keeping 'society's Calibans locked in their caves and beating them back whenever they try to break out'.[9]

The schools are an obvious and easy target. And it may seem legitimate to question the fact that many of them seem to have produced (and continue to produce) large numbers of young people who are not merely ignorant in a formal sense but many of whom seem to lack the personal and collective restraints which society has traditionally expected schools to encourage. It is natural to feel that if schools have failed to discipline – to socialise – their wards, they have failed in their most central and fundamental role. But how can we reasonably expect schools (i.e. hard-pressed, ill-paid and demoralised teachers) to change armies of children and young adults, from homes and communities which are themselves undergoing a complex and unprecedented series of upheavals, into the orderly, well-drilled and malleable young people which is the ideal of many? Even some of the nation's most eminent educational critics consistently fail to recognise the broader social determinants of what teachers can or cannot achieve with their pupils. The concentration upon the relationship between teacher and pupil within the classroom ignores or distorts the even more important social world in which the pupil had to live for the rest of the day.[10]

The move to a national comprehensive school system was not merely a political/educational change but was, at the same time, profoundly influenced by cultural changes which affected the whole western world from the late 1960s onwards. Thus when schools were in a process of organisational transformation they were simultaneously buffeted by forces which, if less easily defined, none the less left permanent marks on the British schooling system. From the late 1960s onwards western society was shaken by a series of interrelated changes; challenges to the *status quo* in every conceivable institution and best remembered by the 'hippie revolution' and the turmoil in universities in Europe and North America. There developed a counter-culture which sought to redefine the structures of everyday (and educational) life and however shortlived many of its extreme manifestations and however bizarre some of the participants' behaviour, they left an influence on western institutions which lasted to the present day. Schools were influenced primarily by the development of a new 'youth culture' but also by the emergence in the profession of progressive younger teachers, influenced by the cultural changes. Cumulatively both these forces converged to challenge the rigid

limits, categories – and roles – within the school systems. Just when
political and formal educational opinion was pressing for
comprehensive schools, the parallel pressure from the counter-
cultural forces eroded other, less tangible divisions; between
teacher and taught, between the sexes and between the hierachies
of knowledge and skills which had characterised earlier education.
School education came to be typified by flexibility and change,
informality and a lack of disciplined hierarchy. Gone was the fairly
rigid world of selected schools and highly structured classes. In their
place, increasingly, there developed a school and classroom culture
which, in allowing a marked degree of self-expression to pupils, in
fact helped to accentuate the conformity to the culture of peer
groups. For many working-class children, this new – and confused –
cultural climate within the schools made it harder to acquire many of
the skills more easily learnt in a more structured system.[11]

Naturally enough, it is easy to exaggerate these points but it is
important to remember that many of the characteristic qualities of
new comprehensive schools derive not so much from formal
educational ideals (though there had been a long pedagogical
tradition of informal self-expression in English educational
thought), but from broader cultural pressures which found a
congenial home in the changing school system. The very concept of
control, of authority and of discipline came to be stigmatised; 'the
culture of unstructured short-run hedonism' was thought
preferable.[12] By the early 1970s this development began to meet
fierce opposition within education with an attempt to roll back the
changes and revert to 'traditional' methods, structures and values.
Often focusing on the empirical data from the new schools (i.e. they
were less academically successful) critics tended to assume that the
schools' flaws and shortcomings were a function primarily of the
new comprehensive schooling system.

Such demands for a reversal of policies had to face a number of
insurmountable problems. First, the new schools were in fact a
brand new system, in place for the unforseeable future and could
not readily be dismantled or restructured after so brief a period.
Secondly, education was beginning to feel the financial effects of
economic decline and political disillusionment with educational
change. But, perhaps more crucial – though less immediately
obvious – was the fact that those schools which displayed the worst
symptoms of the educational malaise complained about were those
in communities which were most acutely troubled by urban renewal

and mounting unemployment. The shortcomings in the school system seemed merely to reflect the broader – and more profound – changes in their host communities. By the time mass un-employment had become an inescapable reality, in the early 1980s, few could seriously argue that changing the school system would make very much difference in communities locked into a tail-spin of urban deprivation, educational inadequacies and a virtual absence of employment prospects. Each of these factors, interrelated as they were, had become elements in a depressingly complex formula, to which few people seemed to have an answer, but which seemed destined to consign successive generations of poorer young citizens to a culture of hopelessness which might find expression in the most outrageous forms of behaviour. For numbers of them, the perfect stages for such performances were the terraces of local football grounds which were relatively easy to control and organise and relatively safe (initially at least) from detection. For many boys and young adults, the football ground was an obvious location for that personal and collective self-expression which, encouraged by the decline of older codes of discipline in almost every other sphere of life they encountered (home, community, school and workplace), could flourish as never before.

Even in the most deprived of urban areas, local schools struggled to try to impose a sense of discipline on their often grudging pupils. But for large numbers of pupils this has the effect of fuelling resistance and resentment rather than instilling an acceptance of discipline. Moreover, for many pupils, school routines – the disciplines of the bell, of teachers' instructions and of the overall timetable – provide a challenge; an organisation and ideal which are to be thwarted as much as obeyed. There is what some investigators have called a 'counter-school culture' which may be little more than a traditional adolescent truculence to an unfriendly regime.[13]

The ability or inability of teachers to establish a 'truce' with truculent pupils has little to do with the nature or quality of education being received; for it is no more than a truce, an acceptance of the *status quo*. But there are many pupils with whom it has proved impossible to negotiate such truces. Generally, the more disruptive pupils are removed to special units. In 1977, there were 239 such units providing 4000 places. Five years later they had increased to 400 units and 7000 places.[14] But even for many of those without such extreme 'behavioural problems' school life is merely a tedious, unlearning rite of passage *en route* to no less tedious labouring work in adult life.[15] What makes the process even more troublesome and the problems of control still more acute is the rise of mass (and particularly regional) unemployment that has severely limited the employment prospect of pupils. However bleak, mindless and repetitive many labouring jobs unquestionably are, they provided more than merely a minimal wage. They offered their own labouring discipline which was itself a beneficiary of the socialisation to which young workers had been exposed in earlier years. In its turn, the work place confirmed and buttressed this discipline by its own codes and practices. Punctuality, time-keeping, persistent application, obedience to orders, the acceptance of rules and conventions within the work place, all these and more were instrumental in securing a labour discipline among the labour force. Of course, we know that the *ideal* labour discipline was rarely in operation and that there are a multitude of ways in which workers can resist or deflect work discipline.[16] Similarly, we need to recall that the ability to avoid the most troublesome aspects of work discipline while simultaneously appearing to conform and abide by its determining rules is a well-tried tradition in a host of labouring occupations. None the less it is widely recognised that one of the major difficulties – and ultimate triumphs – of the earlier generations of industrialists was to shape their labour force into an acceptance – grudging but effective – of the need to accord to labour discipline. Converting labouring people, long-accustomed to different pre-industrial rhythms of labour, to the need to recognise the external disciplines of time, punctuality and application, and to internalise these disciplines, was one of the major achievements of the years of industrial change and development.[17] What has yet to be understood are the consequences for ordered social life (as urban society has known it for a century and a half) when that discipline of labour simply disappears along with work itself.

The formula is thus quite simple – but its consequences potentially explosive. There are in modern England untold thousands of young people in inner cities and decayed industrial communities who have passed through childhood and into adult life untouched by that series of disciplinary agencies so basic to the development of earlier generations of working people. For many of them the disciplines of family and community life have been splintered by urban development; schooling has been similarly transformed and rendered less capable of disciplining its pupils. Finally, the life of labour – unrewarding as it undoubtedly was –

with its attendant and vital codes of labour discipline has vanished into the dust of unemployment.

The evidence of unemployment is readily available; a statistical monument to the collapse of British industry. In 1973 there were only 14 000 school-leavers out of work. In 1980, this had risen to more than one-third of a million – an increase of thirty-fold (and this *despite* an increasing proportion of that age group staying on in education). By the summer of 1982, 926,499 people between the ages of 18 and 25 were unemployed. This is one-sixth of that particular age group; one quarter million of them had been unemployed for a year or more. The problems were even more acute among young people from the ethnic communities, and when the national figures are broken down into local or regional patterns, the evidence for young unemployment is even more alarming. Whereas in 1983, in Liverpool, unemployment stood at 20 per cent, unemployment among those under 18 stood at an almost unbelievable 90 per cent.[18] It was to cater for this catastrophic problem (replicated throughout the country though rarely at such extraordinary levels) that governments since the mid-1970s have established a series of job creation schemes for school-leavers. The purpose was not simply to lower the unemployment figures but, no less important, to revive the obviously flagging discipline to work. The booklet produced by the Manpower Services Commission to help potential employers of these young workers noted the need 'to adjust trainees to normal working conditions' and to check for 'signs of alienation in matters of timekeeping, discipline, etc.'[19] And (though this is not specified) to accept low wages. It is not without its bitter irony that government sought to encourage work discipline – without the essential concomitant of long-term permanent employment.

Yet it is too easy to misunderstand both the problem and government's response to it. It is indisputable that in a world of unemployment the previous disciplines derived from a life of labour simply evaporate. And, to repeat, modern British society has never before confronted the alarming prospect that great swathes of its young urban people are growing into adult life not merely without work but – perhaps more worrying still – devoid of the disciplines so vital to maintaining harmony and social stability. And if proof were required of the dire consequences, many felt that it was necessary only to look to the major urban disturbances of the summer of 1981 and then the Brussels violence to see symptoms of a socially divisive

indiscipline. It is perfectly clear that the links between the two –
between social unrest and the breakdown of old codes of discipline –
are at best circumstantial. We may be able to discover in the
transformation of discipline among certain sections of the young a
broad social phenomenon. More difficult, however, is to prove its
direct effect on specific forms of behaviour.

9 Politics and Sport

For those people who continue to cling to the belief that politics ought to play no part in sport, the aftermath of the Brussels disaster provides an interesting case study. The disaster was an instant diplomatic incident. Prime ministers, Cabinets, Presidents and Ambassadors plunged into a dizzying whirl of political and diplomatic accusations, apologies and accepted responsibilities. Within hours, the British government offered a gift of £250 000 to the victims (having a few days earlier given Bangladesh £50 000 for a cyclone which cost tens of thousands of lives) and the British Prime Minister accepted national responsibility for the actions of a small band of marauding football fans.

The disaster was, for all its unique ferocity and violence, the last straw; the most appalling in a series of violent incidents caused by English fans abroad and which had, so it was felt, damaged the name and reputation of the nation at large. English football violence abroad had proved just *how* politically important the game (like other major sports) really was. The assumed benefits from a close political association with successful sport have long been evident. Now, in 1985, the reverse side to that formula had revealed itself; the association with bad (in this case violent) sport was an unquestioned political liability. The British government rushed to repair the terrible damage; to compensate the victims, to bolster inadequate laws and policing systems, to oblige football authorities to alter their ways and, perhaps most important of all, to be seen (on worldwide TV) to be taking a firm line to restore the nation's image. If anything, the effects of the disaster on Belgium were even more profound, for the subsequent enquiries into the disaster produced a political crisis in the fragile coalition government with the eventual calling of a general election. It requries no great imagination to see that politicians who are normally so eager to be seen at sporting venues, who clearly feel the political benefits to be gained from allying themselves with popular sports, had been damaged by the incident in Brussels.

Sport – of which football is only one, albeit spectacular, example – has traditionally been a highly political phenomenon. Sometimes used by politicians to advance local or sectional interests, sometimes used to promote national or ideological interests (notably at the

Olympics), used even to promote imperial aggrandisement and even political dominance, modern sport has rarely been far from the world of organised politics. International sport in the modern world illustrates the point perfectly. The last two Olympic games (Los Angeles, 1984; Moscow, 1980) were preceded and then characterised by extraordinary political battles between the USSR and the USA. They became in effect a mock battle in which the tangled issues of cold war diplomacy were subsumed within the Olympic movement. The contrasting virtues of Soviet and American life were perhaps the best remembered legacies of those two sporting events. Indeed, the Los Angeles Olympics became not merely an exercise in rampant US nationalism (eddies of which are to be found in most host countries of the games) but a major – and successful – portrayal of the material and human achievements of American life and culture. It was no mere symbol that the most colourful, spectacular, most profitable and most watched of all Olympic games took place in the city associated in the popular mind with the dream factories of films and TV. There were episodes at the 1984 Olympics which belonged more appropriately to Hollywood than to the ideals of Pierre de Coubertin.

The recent history of the Olympic games merely offers a dramatic example of the basic point; that sport and politics have been inextricably linked and have often been mutually interdependent. In any number of widely contrasting historical settings, contemporary sports have been closely tied to political life or, more commonly, have elicited varying responses from the existing political system. In the world of antiquity, athletic competitions were, at once, partly religious, partly political and partly athletic. At its peak, the classical Olympics allowed contemporaries to travel unmolested to the games even through warring communities. Talented – but poor – athletes were sponsored by wealthy patrons and rewarded for their achievements by their city states, though their elevated status and self-esteem did not pass without criticism among Greek authors. Indeed the 'problem' of contemporary athleticism formed a recurring theme in the rich intellectual and philosophical life of ancient Greece. And so important was athleticism that it came to form an important element in the broader study of classical Greek culture.[1] Understandably the Romans borrowed heavily from the Greeks in fashioning their own athletic culture which was, again, not merely a reflection of classical Roman life in its broadest setting but was, throughout, a highly politicised

affair. The organised public games which punctuated the calendar
of Roman life were seen as vital elements in maintaining the peace
and stability, particularly in the capital. It was from this peak of
Roman athleticism that the expression 'bread and circuses' emerged
to become a universal, critical observation on the excesses of
athleticism and their manipulation for political ends. It was said of
the Emperor Trajan, for instance, that 'he well knew that the
excellence of a government is shown no less in care for the
amusements of the people than in serious matters'.[2]

The pattern was much the same throughout the towns of
provincial Rome, for, like Greece, local patrons and politicians were
anxious to use the popular commitment to sports to secure their
own control and maintain the stability of the local area. Moreover, it
was widely believed that many of the sports were ideal training for
ever increasing military demands of the far flung Roman empire.
But the violence of Roman sports was not without its critics who saw
in its bloodshed an agency which debased the public mind and taste
and rendered it uncivilised.[3] The purpose here, in briefly
mentioning the role of sports in the classical world, is simply to
suggest the longevity of the ties between politics and sport. The
feeling that there ought to be a clear divide between the two – that
the two are mutually incompatible – is a relatively *modern* one which
not only flies in the face of contemporary evidence, but equally
conflicts with a tradition which can be readily traced back to the
apogée of the classical sporting tradition.

From the early days of the modern history of football the game
had obvious and undeniable political ramifications. The ancient
traditional game had been equally political in a number of important
ways. The folk game of football, often enshrined in certain Shrove
Tuesday rituals, was at once denounced for the mayhem attendant
on the turbulent games, played largely by youths and young men,
and yet also used for good social reasons. Like European carnivals,
the games of football (and other recreations) which dotted the
recreational and religious calendar of English folk customs were,
like many of the classical sporting occasions, sanctioned and
approved as a means of maintaining control. Such an explanation is
too crude to do full justice to the range of motives and reactions
which shaped responses to the games of football (which were
themselves primarily local) in late medieval and early modern
England. Still it is true to say that football – which was often
turbulent, violent and socially disruptive – was disliked in direct

proportion to its threats to social harmony, and yet approved of to the degree that it could be used to channel youthful energies and aggressions into acceptable forms and on specific occasions.

The game was particularly disliked by religious opinion which objected not merely to its godless qualities of youthful excess but more especially because it so often infringed the Sabbath. This became a serious problem for the game – along with a host of other recreations – in the years of Puritan ascendancy in the sixteenth and seventeenth centuries. In the words of Phillip Stubbes (1583): 'Any exercise which withdraweth us from godliness, either upon the Sabbath or any other day, is wicked and to be forbidden.'[4] Most strident in those years, this religious objection to football (and games in general) became even more influential in the nineteenth century with the emergence of a powerful sabbatarian lobby, devoted to keeping the Sabbath holy and to preventing both the continuation of traditional recreation and the development of new ones. What made such objections so important were those changes in society at large which transformed the physical face of Britain. The development of an increasingly industrial and a highly urbanised society not only accumulated a growing proportion of the people into urban areas but imposed on them the newly shaped disciplines of industrial and urban living. The week was consumed by the demands of the work place (itself increasingly – but not uniquely – dominated by the machine) and the waking day was consumed by unremitting labour – measured out by the clock – in a way which left little time for rest and recreation.[5] Working people found themselves with less free time and fewer spare days on which to relax, a trend aided by the insistence of early industrialists and urban politicians that work – not leisure – should determine the lives of the labour force. Clearly, such a general and sweeping account must do an injustice to the exceptions and variations to the overall pattern.

The basic point to stress is that recreations and leisure – of which the game of football was only one of many forms – became an important political issue in the early nineteenth century. Arguments about free time, urban space and recreational facilities, about the relationship between enjoyment, relaxation and social stability were important political issues throughout the last century. In the last quarter of that century there had developed, partly as a result of those arguments, but also, perhaps primarily, as a function of the nation's changing economy, a wide range of popular cultural forms and entertainments which had mass support, were commercial in structure and which had been, from the first, closely tied to political and social argument. Music halls, seaside resorts, football stadiums – these were merely the most obvious of a myriad of innovations in popular leisure which had transformed the social life of Britain by the turn of the century.[6]

In the case of football, politicians – national and local – were quick to seize on the potential benefits of associating themselves with local clubs and with the national game. Indeed, national politicians joked among themselves in Parliament, about attending important football matches. Lord Rosebery remarked, in 1899: 'We all feel it is not a light sacrifice which the leader of the House of Commons makes in giving up his Saturday half-holiday, so hardly earned, to come and perform the duty he has performed today.' Mr Balfour replied, 'I can assure him and you that there is no better way of spending a Saturday afternoon than that which we have enjoyed.'[7] They were referring to the FA Cup Final at Crystal Palace. Two factors explain this alliance of politicians and football. First, among the well-educated and prosperous MPs, football had been a major part of their recreational activities; they had learned to enjoy it as schoolboys, had come to accept its social and physical virtues and, naturally enough, continued to like it in adult life. But the game was equally important for more direct, political reasons. In an urban and now highly democratic society, the activities of the male electorate were of immediate political relevance for MPs of all persuasions. For politicians of a humbler station, football had also been important, not merely in a childhood, community game but also, from the 1880s onwards, a major ingredient in the education provided for boys in the new elementary schools. Thus it was that most politicians of varied social origins were naturally attracted to the game of their childhood and adolescence.

Others were naturally drawn to the game, notably local businessmen and entrepreneurs keen not only to capitalise on the money-making abilities of the expansive and commercial game but keen too to gain that indefinable credit (with its commercial spin-offs) of being associated with the game. Time and again, the new professional clubs were launched or expanded by businessmen/politicians anxious to build a monument to their own achievements; custom-built stadiums which were the pride of the town and into which teemed unprecedented crowds of paying spectators week after week. From the first then local politicians and businessmen were closely associated with the development of the modern professional game. In the following century the pattern was to remain much the same. In the 1880s, as in the 1980s, powerful and wealthy men used their influence and cash to establish, develop (or more recently, to salvage) a local club. Many of the prominent teams were created by the energies and efforts of such men; Manchester United, Liverpool and West Ham are just some of the more famous examples.[8]

Ironically, professional football was not always a lucrative investment. The initial development of a club – buying prime urban land, the cost of constructing the stadium, players' wages and running costs (meagre as they may now seem), all required heavy investments long before income could be guaranteed. And, of course, that income, from spectators, depended substantially on the footballing fortunes of the team itself.[9] Football, for those local political magnates who turned to it in its early stages of growth (1880–1914), offered a much less certain form of investment than a host of other contemporary commercial speculations. And yet, then as more recently, the financial uncertainties of the game did not repel interested parties. Indeed, if we examine the longer span of footballing history in Britain, the game has throughout been characterised by a marked degree of economic irrationality. The prospects of better investments elsewhere has rarely deterred a certain type of magnate; one with money to spare, anxious to place himself in the public eye and to gain local prestige and fame. There were then certain indefinable but none the less important invisible economic and political benefits to be gained from a high-profile involvement with local clubs. Magnates and politicians were guaranteed a degree of regular publicity and acclaim which in the normal course of events would have cost them considerable money and canvassing efforts. Of course, the reverse side of the formula is also true. In times of difficulties – when a club's footballing fortunes were in decline – the financial and political benefits were less certain. Nevertheless, local – and national – worthies continued to maintain their footballing connections. It became an act of major public benefaction for a local magnate to step in and solve an ailing club's fortunes.

There was a sense in which football – like other games and leisure pursuits – were thought to be apolitical, or rather were often viewed as harmless diversions which ought to remain unsullied by conventional political links. But it is perfectly clear that from its earliest days football (and other sports) came to occupy an important social function which was political in a number of key regards. Among those in educational and political authority, sports – of which football was the most important – came to be regarded as a key element in the smooth and efficient functioning of a mature, urban industrial society.[10] Indeed, it was one of *the* major intellectual transformations in the course of the nineteenth century that popular sport came to be viewed not as disruptive – the solvent of social tranquillity – but as an important element in the complex formula for maintaining social order. In some respects, the mass sports of the late nineteenth century, promoted most effectively through the new school system, were often viewed much as the recreations of classical Rome were regarded; as a safety valve which tapped the otherwise potentially troublesome energies of the masses. Clearly, it would be misleading to claim that the mass recreations of the late century were mere bread and circuses. But it is undoubtedly true that there was a distinct political view of mass, organised sports which saw them in this beneficial light, and which sought to encourage them for that reason.

Football was political in other respects. The widespread acceptance of the game as an important element in the compulsory education of the nation's young (males at least) involved an educational perception of the role of organised sports which had obvious and admitted political ramifications. The game had important instrumental consequences among the working-class young – those boys who would grow up into the future labour force. It encouraged an emphasis on physical fitness which, it was argued, countered a number of the debilitating consequences of plebeian life in deprived urban circumstances. Equally it involved the development of a sense of team play – a commitment on the part of individuals to subsume their own interests to that of the team. Part of the ethos of team play was the unquestioned acceptance of authority; obedience to the orders of captain, schoolmaster or anyone in immediate team authority. Football was a game which, increasingly, was hedged around with rules and regulations; it came to represent an extraordinary ediface of codification and authority, enshrined in written rules and conventions which had to be accepted unquestioningly, and contravention of which involved immediate and long-term punishments.

Such structures of regulation are, of course, so commonplace in the modern western world, at every level we care to examine, that we tend not to notice them; to imagine that it is natural and traditional. In fact, it is relatively modern – a recent intrusion of the evermore complex bureaucracy of a modern western society. Football and sports at large were only one aspect of the increasingly regulated world of the later nineteenth and early twentieth century. But sport was extremely important in securing among successive generations of working-class boys an acceptance of codes of conduct and discipline which were important in themselves and, perhaps more crucially, as an element in the broader discipline required of the labour force. There are quite obviously limits to this argument. Not all boys accepted the discipline of the sporting ethic, and not all carried their sports discipline beyond the sports field. Moreover, sport was only one arena in which the values of rigid discipline were inculcated. They were, obviously, to be found in operation within the family, the school classroom, the work place, in the local community (itself hedged in by social conventions as much as legal restraints) and in a host of private institutions – churches, chapels, Sunday schools and the like. Yet this is not to deny the parallel importance of that discipline which was peculiar to sport and which, in many respects, seemed all the more important because it became an unconscious element in what was, for many participants, an enjoyable experience.

Conversely, however, it is unlikely that the discipline of codified sports could have been truly effective without the other converging disciplines of working-class life at large. This latter point was to become more evident in recent years when the corrosion of older disciplines – in schools, work place and home – left sport exposed as one of the few surviving institutions which continued to demand of its participants an unswerving loyalty to and an unquestioning acceptance of its codes, conventions and punishments. Not surprisingly, young footballers (or tennis players for that matter) bridle at these demands when, in almost every other aspect of their social and economic lives, the nature of discipline – of authority and obedience – has changed so fundamentally.

Football was then political in the broadest sense; as an element in the politically determined development of the education of working-class males in the first two generations of compulsory schooling. Boys from more prosperous homes, attending private schooling, were subject to the no less disciplined attachment to sport, but with a different purpose in mind. Theirs was to be a future of leadership, at all levels of English life and for which the sporting ethic was no less important. But it was among their social inferiors that sport was used to inculcate the corresponding values of obedience. It was no accident that men in political authority at the turn of the century were as happy to see the widespread acceptance of football among the plebeian young as their forebears had been miserable, a century before, to see the older, indisciplined games persist among the common people. With sports pacified and regulated, they were given the seal of political approval and actively promoted for the good of the individual and the nation at large. The contrast with 1985 could not be harsher.

So far, the concentration of this chapter has been on the specifically local and British dimension of sporting and footballing politics. There is, however, another, and in many respects, more significant political dimension to the game. Football – like many other sports – quickly became an issue of international political and diplomatic importance. Once the game had established itself as the national game, with all the benefits thought to flow from it, football took on an international dimension. The game was rapidly transplanted around the globe by Britons travelling, trading or settling abroad. Long before the First World War football had become a feature of urban life throughout western Europe, with the replication of teams, leagues, competitions and, eventually, international competition between clubs and later international teams. The first international games, between England and Scotland, offered a foretaste of what was to follow; of the game transformed into highly emotional – albeit artificial – contests of rival nationalism. Such games – attracting massive, and passionately partisan crowds – were themselves instrumental in whipping up a heady feeling of crude national fervour and its corollary, an even cruder zenophobia.

By the late nineteenth century it was widely accepted that sport had become an instrument of international concern and could, if properly used, be helpful in promoting international accord and understanding. It was in fact this feeling that persuaded the French aristocrat, Baron de Coubertin, to initiate the modern Olympic movement in 1896. Coubertin was deeply influenced by the ideal of public school athleticism, with its belief in selfless commitment to the team and the relegation of individual interest and ambition to the greater good of the team. It seemed to many that such an ideal (however remote it might be from sporting reality – even within the public schools) was a perfect vehicle for promoting peace and goodwill among nations, more so at a time of mounting European international rivalries in the 1890s. Unlike other sports – notably athletics and cricket – English football was reluctant to involve itself too closely in international affairs – on or off the field – before 1914.[11] Even between the wars the game was characterised by a reluctance among men of authority in football's upper circles to pay too much attention to the game abroad (with serious consequences for the competitive edge of the national game). None the less more English national and club teams began to play abroad, a fact which inevitably had political and diplomatic repercussions. Governments of the day came to see travelling footballers as ambassadors for their country and to pay attention to the preparation, conduct and outcome of footballing visits abroad.

After 1918 sport was promoted even more vigorously by the state, primarily through enhanced educational provision within schools. But it was the rise of fascist regimes in Italy and Germany which revealed to anyone with eyes to see the extraordinary degree to which sport – and soccer – had become political tools to be manipulated and organised for the good of the state. Obviously this was much more striking in the totalitarian regimes of the 1920s and 1930s – and was to become equally pronounced among Eastern block nations after the Second World War.[12] But the excesses and overt political involvement of totalitarian regimes in their nation's sports, and their use of sports to enhance national and political prestige ought not to deceive us about the escalating political and diplomatic importance of sports in democratic societies. There is an abundance of evidence in recent history (and contemporary life) to illustrate the point. The famous MCC 'bodyline' cricket tour of Australia in 1932–3, the development of Gaelic sports as a branch of Irish nationalism,[13] the insistence that the English soccer team, playing in Berlin in 1936, raise their arms in the fascist salute to Hitler[14] – these and a host of other major and minor overtly political examples illustrate the basic proposition that sport was becoming increasingly political in proportion to its increased internationalism after 1918.

This was a tendency which continued, at an even faster pace, after the Second World War. To a marked degree, the ever increasing importance attached to international sport is but one aspect of the transformation in leisure pursuits over the past thirty years. Much of that transformation is a direct result of economic change, as ever more people found themselves able to afford the new and more varied commercial pleasures of advanced industrial societies. Equally the major technological changes (cheap air travel, universal telecommunications) have revolutionised most recreations. In the case of soccer, it became commonplace from the late 1950s for teams and their fans to travel throughout Europe, while millions at home could watch the games on TV. In that same period there has been a massive proliferation of international competitions which have, in many respects, become more important to the ambitions and finances of many football clubs than their domestic commitments. From the first these competitions began to change the nature and thrust of the game's sporting edge. Clubs and teams whose activities had been specifically local or regional in appeal and character gradually became charged with international commitments. Not merely content to defeat their local rivals, English (and other British) teams were now involved in the pursuit of *national* success; they carried their country's name and fortunes with them throughout Europe (and in the national team's case, around the world). More often than not such games became contests between nations, an image actively portrayed (often in bizarre, crude terms) by the popular press. Frequently English teams abroad represented much more than their home towns. The overt nationalism of such forays were made all the more blatant by the widespread use of the Union Jack by travelling supporters. Successes were often greeted with exaggerated outbursts of national fervour, defeats (much more common) initiated mournful inquests into the collapse not merely of national sporting prowess but also into the broader difficulties of the nation at large. The failure of English teams (and the behaviour of their fans) came to be viewed as a symbolic guide to the spiralling misfortunes of the English people. And yet the closer the association was drawn – between sporting and national fortunes – the more acute was the disappointment when English teams failed to live up to the (often exaggerated) expectations demanded of them. Of course, it is also true that a number of clubs – notably Liverpool – were exceptionally successful. But in years of national self-doubt and economic gloom, far too much value came to be attached to the achievements of those few bearers of English prestige abroad who could succeed against foreign rivals.

Politicians had been eager to associate themselves with sporting (and football) success, and to benefit from the inevitable consequential publicity. Famous players, the major stars, were courted, successful teams were entertained, prominent managers and personalities in the game were honoured and decorated. It may be true that football was late in being recognised in this way – that honours and political favour had been bestowed on other games much earlier – but from the 1960s onwards football received more than its fair share of political adulation. It is perfectly true that much of the political cultivation of football and footballers stemmed from an undeniable love of the game, but it also seems reasonable to claim that there was political capital to be gained from this well-publicised affair. Not unlike a century before, the liaison between local and national politicians and football (and other games, too, of course) was of political advantage to people who needed to keep their name and image in the public eye. This became more striking as football was given increasing coverage on television and as the game (and sport in general) began to occupy a greater coverage in the popular press and even to creep from the sports pages on to the news pages. The game – with its extraordinarily high public profile and its ubiquitous presentation in print and on television – had become an irresistible temptation to politicians of all parties whose careers, popularity and futures, depended as never before on their ability to project themselves to the viewing public.

Football was not unique in offering such a platform to politicians but, unlike other sports, football began to prove itself a mixed blessing from the late 1960s. The game became an indisputable social problem, its fans causing trouble and creating havoc throughout urban England during the football season. Crowd behaviour – and the football clubs' reaction to it – demanded a political response, or rather a series of responses, which began to lure politicians into an entirely new and unprecedented relationship with the game. Parliament became the forum in which the game's problems were debated – problems which, as this book has already shown, spilled far beyond the strictly parochial and limited problems of the game itself. Football seemed to be the focus for a convergence of major social ills, all of which were politically contentious and which, when they came together, raised worrying questions about the very tranquillity and future development of English urban life. Clearly, football was not the *cause* of these manifold social problems. But it was inescapable that it had become the *occasion* and place where many of these difficult matters seemed to erupt in a particularly nasty and inescapable fashion.

Thus it was that the Brussels disaster, while being an utterly unpredictable accident, had an element of inevitability about it. So volatile had English fans become – and so precarious the power of authority to contain them – that it seemed but a matter of time or place before English fans spilled beyond control with unimaginable consequences. It was no less predictable that politicians should be dragged into the fray; long unable to persuade footballing authorities to control their fans, or to impose their own solutions, the government of the day was obliged to step in. And in doing so instantly, in taking national responsibility for the disaster, the government was obliged to respond with heavy draconian measures. The game which once brought such prestige, prominence and fame had now become a damaging liability; a shame and a disability to government and nation alike. The measures which inevitably followed were designed both to curb a social problem but, equally, to strike a political posture; to leave no one in any doubt that government had set its face against such publically damaging behaviour.

10 Epilogue: The Changing Face of Britain

The diasters of 1985 prompted a detailed enquiry not simply into the whys and wherefores of the events themselves, but into the very nature of contemporary British life. Critics at home and abroad set out to answer the question, what had changed in British life to make such horrible events possible? The first – deceptive – response was that these events reflected not on Britain but more specifically on England. North of the border, there was a complacent affirmation that the troubles had nothing to do with Scotland. In a sense this was obviously true. But the emphasis on the recent pacification of Scottish football fans within their own grounds ignores the continuing problem of their misbehaviour when travelling (especially to England) and the incidents involving Scottish fans abroad. If the ire of public feeling – and of football's authorities – was directed, quite properly, at England it would take a mealy mouthed nationalism to imagine that the basic problems had been solved elsewhere in Britain.

At times – then and since – it was not always easy to see the links between a disastrous fire and a riot in a distant country. A more detailed study of the game's history suggests, however, that the links are there, if indirect. Yet it is also true that these two events were fortuitous, contingent episodes. They were, at one level, terrible accidents; unintended and unforseen misfortunes visited on utterly innocent people. Clearly, they *could* have been avoided – but so too could many other human disasters. Yet, it will be countered, if they were indeed mere accidents – acts of God – how can any amount of detailed long-term social analysis help to explain them?

Perhaps one of the most interesting features of the immediate debate about these disasters was the fact that commentators (almost universally) assumed that they were to be explained not by the immediate, local sociological explanations. Time and time again, in that plethora of articles which appeared in the early summer of 1985, authors simply assumed that the disasters, particularly at Brussels, were historically determined. Indeed, this basic fact is a remarkable testament to the degree to which social inquiry has been shaped by a popular sociological tradition which is itself historically rooted. The danger with such an approach is that it naturally involves a temptation – to which most observers succumbed – to impose on the outcome an inexorable inevitability; to see the disasters of 1985 as the unfolding of irresistibly long-term trends. There was an equal danger of writing not so much an account of the disasters themselves but offering a history of contemporary Britain which neatly culminates in, and therefore explains, the events of 1985.

It would, at one level, be absurd to detach the events of 1985 from the immediate historical context. Although historians tend to view the recent past as the preserve not of historians but of social scientists, it is clearly important to come to grips with these changes over the past twenty-five years which form the determining background without which any understanding of recent events will be partial and inadequate. In that period, a host of converging changes served to transform British urban life in general and, more especially for our interests, the nature and role of football. In the process there was a marked transformation in the relationship between the game – for so long the undisputed national game – and the people who have traditionally formed its basic support. Indeed, the game of football has changed more rapidly and substantially over the past twenty-five years than in any comparable period since its inception a century ago. How could it be otherwise since those same years were marked by extraordinary transformations in British urban life at large? The very face of urban Britain has been utterly transformed in that period, at a pace and with a thoroughness which at times threatened to match the revolutionary process of urbanisation in the nineteenth century. Nowhere was this more dramatically the case than in the old industrial and working-class heartlands of Britain. Those industries – and their labour force – which formed the bedrock of British economic pre-eminence in the years up to 1914 simply withered and decayed, first before a complex global economic process and then, from the late 1970s, under the pressure of governmental policies.

The convergence of accidental, capricious decline and that positively encouraged by recent government policy, led not only to major economic change in Britain and abroad but to dramatic physical changes in the urban environment. Great swathes of industry and working-class communities were simply obliterated by the transforming zeal of urban renewal, slum clearance and, later, by industrial decline. Much of the inspiration behind the destruction of older communities was a social and political optimism

– the belief that what took the place of the old, decayed communities was a major and qualitative improvement in the material and social lives of working people. But that optimism was to be quickly and thoroughly disabused. The experiments at social engineering which created new towns, transformed sections of old towns and which laid waste to acres of urban life, created as many problems as they cured or modified. Chunks of population were relocated, uprooted from those communities which had for long shaped their personal and collective social life.

Much of the desire to change the living environment for working people was informed by a commitment to improving the undoubtedly wretched material conditions of life. Ever since the early 1950s, the gradual improvements registered in the material conditions of British life had changed not only the obvious, physical world at large but, equally important, had enhanced the expectations which people held of the world around them. So many of the material objects, and patterns of life, which had long been acceptable to earlier generations were, by the early 1960s, found to be inadequate by more and more people. Few aspects of social and economic life remained immune to this elevation of expectations; life within the home, the nature of work and its rewards, family life itself – all of these and more changed quite markedly. And so too, inevitably, did the way many people spend their leisure hours. Those leisure pursuits which had once been unquestioned and which were thought to be natural and automatic now faced critical scrutiny from the challenges posed by competing and, to many people, more attractive alternatives. Just as the home and the community changed before the initially seductive appeal of 'modernisation', so too did the patterns of enjoyment and organised pleasures. These changes are so obvious because they are so recent: foreign travel, DIY, television and car ownership. In fact the changes in leisure patterns in the past generation represent some of the more fundamental and striking changes in modern social life.

In the midst of all this change, football remained oddly unmoving. Although it is true that the game has been altered in certain key respects, it is the game's unchanging organisational shape and geographic location which form a direct link to the early days of the modern game. But these same abiding features have also isolated the game not only from transformations in urban life at large, but more especially from those communities which the clubs and the teams once served. This point is obvious to any casual visitor to most professional English grounds. So many of those grounds are decrepit architectural reminders of former pleasures – museum pieces to the way people once tolerated spartan conditions for their leisure pursuits. Often, the immediate community around the football ground is not only poor – rows of inner city terraced housing in congested streets – but sometimes the local community is ethnic. The composition and nature of the neighbouring community is generally quite different from those which traditionally supported the clubs. This means that when local fans arrive for a game they generally travel to the ground from other parts of the town – or from much further afield. Indeed, the local communities often *dread* the arrival of fans and board up house and home against any potential threat or damage. This contrast is even sharper where the fans are white and the local community is Asian or black. The old geographic ties – between local fans and local teams – have quite clearly been severed by the demographic shifts in urban life and by the revolution in transportation and car ownership which have eased personal movement between and within urban communities. Clearly the patterns of recent support for football enshrine their own distinctive rituals but they are, for all that, quite different rituals from those of early generations of football fans. Nowhere is this sense of isolation – between local community and club – more striking than in those cases where the locals are Asian. Local people in their own traditional dress, watch uncomprehendingly as coachloads of whites arrive flaunting extravagant hair and clothes, often fighting each other or the police, to watch this strange game of football.

As we have already seen, the racial dimension to the modern game is very complex and confusing. But whatever its form, it represents graphically the changing nature of urban life. Many clubs now find themselves hemmed in, physically, by ethnic communities which show little or no concern about their progress and fate – save to fear the arrival of the fans. Professional teams can now boast a number of black players (though it is interesting that most of those players come from West Indian or African origins and not from Asian communities). Yet while many teams can boast of their black players, they regularly run a gauntlet of racial abuse. Even here, though, the pattern is unclear, for local black players can be cheered, visiting blacks abused. Sometimes this racist abuse seems to be related to activities organised in and around the ground by extremist and racist political groups. This racial tension is only the most unpleasant of a series of offensive features of the modern professional football game. Like the gross obscenities chanted at visitors, referees (and even at distant objects of local antagonisms), the racism to be heard on modern grounds is clearly not an isolated phenomenon; it is not a peculiar or distinctive creation of football itself. Rather, it has found in football an ideal vehicle and occasion for its virulent and offensive expression. Nurtured by the demographic changes in urban life and exacerbated by the catastrophic economic decline of the past decade, such public outbursts of racism may well be a minority occupation. But such racism clearly survives because of the tolerance displayed towards it by public and private organisations. To put the matter boldly, so little has been done (in this case by football clubs and organisations) to combat racial abuse that it has thrived in the atmosphere of general indifference or inactivity.

It is impossible not to notice the racism and obscenities at football grounds. They are chanted in shrill unison by groups of young men, whose collective abuse is audible throughout the stadium and is readily picked up by radio and TV microphones. Try as they might, broadcasting engineers cannot always mask such obscenities which inevitably float into the nation's living rooms. And if the sound fails to get through, abusive (though sometimes funny) placards and banners often make similar points. The end result of all this – the work of small but well-drilled groups – is a general atmosphere of menace and unpleasantness. Yet this is not always the case – and not always true even of the worst clubs. There survives, somehow, that fund of stoicism and good humour among fans which can often produce moments of extraordinary collective mirth and amiable banter. Here again, there is a risk of romanticising these qualities and seeing them driven out by more recent and much nastier social forces. None the less, modern grounds have become unpleasant and threatening where they were once merely austere and uninviting.

It would be quite wrong to suggest that such a climate has been created by the ubiquitous presence of television. On the other hand, it is unrealistic to discuss what has happened to the modern game without some recognition of the seminal influence of television on all those involved in the game; fans, players and management. Clearly television is in many respects an innocent bystander, but in certain key respects it has come to shape and alter behaviour and this is merely a specific illustration of the incalculable influence it has come to play in the western world. The difficulty here for any critic of the contemporary game is to place the role of television alongside a host of other factors which have changed the modern game. It is obviously insufficient to suggest that any one factor is *the* prime agent of change. In the case of crowd behaviour, no one could convincingly argue that television alone is responsible for much of the more outrageous gang warfare that takes place around the football clubs. Those gangs whose prime ambition is to take on and assault the opposing team's gangs do so away from the public gaze (though often using the vocabulary of the game itself to describe their tactics and achievements). But in the initial phase, when gangs were gaining a tentative foothold in the stadiums, their activities and their ambitions were given instant national coverage (and consequent credit in the activists' eyes) by the presence of television cameras. Present to record and transmit a sporting event, television became the means for the transformation of a local and specific phenomenon into a national problem.

By the 1980s, however, the misbehaviour of key sectors of football crowds had become an autonomous and self-sustaining force. With its own codes, vocabulary, its own rules and structure, clothing and leaders, the football gang has all the characteristics of urban gangs. The major innovation was that they were attached, in ways not always clear to outsiders, to certain football teams. In a sense this was very much like the territorial attachments and battles of youth gangs in a number of other cultures. But the host body – football – found itself utterly bewildered by the development; transfixed and incapable of effective controlling measures. There were, it is true, a number of successes, for some of the major clubs were able (logistically and – most importantly – financially) to impose a strict regime of control and supervision on their grounds, all in co-operation with the local police. The end result is – at the safer, more secure grounds – a police presence and a degree of crowd control the likes of which have never before been seen at football clubs. Stadiums have been expensively adapted to aid this process. In fact without certain costly modifications to the physical plant, effective control is often impossible. Again, we return to the central question of finance. If grounds can only be made secure for spectators by expensive alterations, what are those unprofitable clubs – and the very great majority of them are losing money – to do? The end result is a rather pathetic spectacle; these Victorian institutions, the clubs, begging for public or state funds to bring themselves up to levels of safety long expected of other public institutions. And all in order to safeguard fans who are turning away from the game in their thousands. The obvious answer – brutal and offensive to that admirable ingrained sense of history which informs the British attachment to traditional institutions – is that those clubs incapable of bringing themselves up to date must simply cease to exist in their present form. It is perfectly true that a number of clubs have suitably changed themselves to confront these problems. And it is with those grounds in mind that some people have claimed that the Heysel disaster would have been unlikely to have happened in England. The obvious retort is that people also lost their lives at Bradford and Birmingham.

Throughout the broad discussion about what to do with football hooliganism, the drift of the debate has been towards control and policing. If, as the accumulating evidence suggests, certain football gangs have a hard-core leadership whose commitment to their gang and its fighting is fanatical and unflinching, then the problem is indeed one of control – of vigorous and effective policing. Equally, if this scenario is comprehensively accurate, it is not evident that many of the alleged causes of gang misbehaviour are very relevant. Unemployment is not obviously an issue among those young men, fully employed, who spend all their money travelling to football matches; drink might not be a factor among those gang leaders who are insistent on keeping a clear head for the day's nasty activities. But even this acknowledgement of the existence of a hard, vicious leadership at the heart of football gangs will not fully explain *all* the trouble at the grounds. There are eddies of misbehaviour – in the stadiums and *en route* to and from them which involve more than simply the gangs. A climate has developed which permits and even encourages outlandish and outrageous behaviour among young fans – secure among the crowds of their own peers – but which falls short of the viciousness of organised gangs. It is among this broader body of younger fans that many of the other explanatory factors may well be important – drink most notably. Yet here, as in much of what has been said so far, it is not clear that any satisfactory explanation will come from studying the game itself – from the history and sociology of football *tout court*. Indeed, in writing this book, the author has been influenced as much by researches conducted on peripheral or tangental issues as by work undertaken specifically on the game itself. We are, once more, thrown back on to a much more widely based analysis which seeks to locate the specific problems of the game within a broad historical and sociological framework.

Such an approach runs a number of risks. First, it will unquestionably confront a hostile, populist reaction which interprets any attempt to explain a major social problem as an attempt to justify it. Even the language normally used for social analysis can provoke ridicule in the popular press. To a degree this is an understandable response to the confusing and opaque language often used in social analysis. But it also reflects that anti-intellectualism of British life which raises its head whenever social problems are publicly debated in words of more than two syllables. Nor is this response restricted to the tabloids or to the ubiquitous 'man in the street'; it can be heard echoing round Senior Common Rooms of universities throughout the land, notably among academics who feel so scornful of the social sciences. But this populist hostility also derives in part from a national attachment to 'common sense' and from the feeling that people can readily spot and recognise misbehaviour when they see it and will demand speedy, well-tried punishments for the perpetrators. At this level we drift back to that incohate sense of unhappiness shared by many older people that the rise of difficult modern social problems seems to be in proportion to the number of social observers studying them and what is basically required is the firm smack of policing and punishment. Time and again, serious studies of football's problems have been greeted by scornful public dismissal and by the related demand for harsh reprisals on trouble-makers. It is not to claim a reprieve for wrong-doers to suggest both that we need to know why people behave as they do and that we need to cast our gaze more broadly and not to focus uniquely on the game of football itself.

The immediate results of the disasters of 1985 are already with us, notably an increasingly harsh regulation and control of the game and its supporters by outside agencies. New laws, Home Office scrutiny, ever more intrusive policing and even, possibly, restrictions on entry to grounds; all these are currently in operation and threaten to be more vigorously applied. Many of the consequent intrusions on individual liberties are quite severe (intrusions which those same people would not tolerate in other walks of life), but which are thought to be necessary to prevent further excesses. Many fans – and casual spectators – naturally bridle at the searches, marshalling and threats of policemen at football grounds. And there are few professional games where ordinary – and innocent – fans fail to find themselves unjustly treated by the local police. But this is perhaps the inevitable price the innocent have to pay for the prevention of absurd behaviour by an ill-intentioned minority. It is in a sense part of that Benthamite balance obvious in other areas of society; of weighing the virtues of peace and control against the vices of a loss of liberty and self-interest.

Equally it seems plausible to claim that this acceptance of a more intensive policing system is part of a broader intervention by the police and the state in order to secure the safety and peace of the public at large. This was true, in a spectacular fashion in the miners' strike of 1984–5 and it is true at a less notable level in the way people tolerate searches of personal items when entering public places. Indeed, fewer and fewer people object to – or even notice – such intrusive scrutiny (officials peering into handbags, searching one's clothing) because it has become so commonplace in modern western life (notably, in Britain, as a deterrent to possible terrorism). It may seem to many readers a little far-fetched to place the policing of the modern football ground in this context. Yet this is surely where it belongs; as part of a tradition which has developed since the late 1960s, in Britain, of increasingly intrusive policing and the consequent (though often unnoticed and unremarked) loss of personal freedoms. Some people may not feel it unusual for police to ask men to remove their boots before entering a football stadium; a generation ago it would have been thought outrageous. Even earlier it would have precluded most men wanting to watch the game. Many might feel it unexceptional to keep visiting fans detained in a stadium for an hour after the final whistle in order to be able to guide them safely through the deserted streets after the game. Not long ago such policing – however much in the interests of the visitors – would have been unthinkable.

On top of these general policing methods there is an indefinable but extremely important climate of tolerance for arbitrary police intrusions. Time and again individual or small groups of policemen, admittedly facing a difficult and often unpleasant task, take matters into their own hands against fans and young people whose antics or words are merely the outbursts of innocuous enthusiasm. Fans ejected for merely chanting their team's name, fans whose personal property is confiscated or destroyed, these and other instances may seem insignificant and irrelevant when set against the undeniable problems of policing the modern football ground. But it would take a partisan opaqueness to reality (of the kind traditionally displayed by the Police Federation) to deny that the policing of modern football grounds has come to involve a degree of police intrusion and arbitrariness, with a consequent diminution of personal liberties, which would have shocked earlier generations. Perhaps this is, to repeat, merely another – and inevitable – aspect of the encroachment of the modern state into previously inviolable areas of personal and collective life. It is, moreover, all the more difficult to resist when the alternative – in this case the violence and mayhem witnessed in 1985 – is even more outrageous. There is little credit – in the aftermath of the Heysel disaster – to be gained by standing up and denouncing the consequent invasions of liberties proposed in bringing football fans under control. Such a plan would fly in the face of a populist British acceptance of harsh and often arbitrary measures against potential wrong-doers. To query the justice of measures aimed at crowd control is to run the risk of appearing to side with the proponents of outrageous acts of violence and criminality.

This is especially the case in the political climate of Britain in the mid-1980s, in which organised violence has posed serious threats to stability (in the miners' strike and, most spectacularly, in the bomb attack against the majority of the Cabinet). In a troubled society beset by a host of profound social ills and in which outbursts or threats of violence seem to have become endemic, there is little personal or political credit to be gained by resisting or denouncing the encroachment of the state and of its policing agencies. Indeed, the very fact that we can legitimately talk about this broader problem when ostensibly studying the game of football is itself an indication of the extent to which the state has successively intruded itself – albeit to safeguard the interests of the majority of its members.

If any single feature has characterised the response to the disasters of 1985 it is surely confusion. Inside and outside the game, at home and abroad, the response to what happened was one of bafflement; bafflement that such things could happen among the English. This was equally true after the urban riots of 1981 – and again after the Birmingham riots of 1985. All three episodes of collective violence – different as they unquestionably were – raised disturbing questions in the minds of people accustomed to thinking of England as a peaceable, well-ordered and unflappable nation. And it is true that such outbursts do indeed run against the current of recent (though not long-term) history. It has become part of the English people's self-perception – and the image they have carefully cultivated abroad – that they are a nation of peaceable people, slow to anger and able to conduct their social lives without the turbulent excesses of others. This is, obviously, a caricature to a degree but it is a caricature which has served a host of social and political purposes, at home and abroad. And it ignores a contrary dimension to English history, touched upon elsewhere in this book. None the less, it is the case that the violent outbursts of the 1980s do seem to run counter to a peaceable tradition which stretches back a century and a half. What adds to the confused response in 1985 is the suspicion that such acts of violence will become more frequent, indeed unavoidable.

Time and again, one reaction to the troubles of 1985 is that Britain can expect more of them; the reason so often given (in, for instance, the letter column of *The Times*) is the appalling social and economic state of the nation. Thus the arguments come full circle. Even people who find it hard to see the direct causal links between, say, the violence in Brussels and broad social matters are equally clear that it would be absurd to divorce that violence from society's problems at large. And here critics of vastly conflicting political and social outlooks come together. The very great majority of those who expressed views on the disasters of 1985 sought to locate their own distinctive explanation in broad social and economic trends. And it is at this point that so much confusion arises. First, and as we have suggested throughout the book, the links between those trends and what happened at Brussels (and even more often within English stadiums) is less clear than many might initially claim. Secondly – and this is the most perplexing issue – scrutiny of contemporary English society reveals a society in a process of rapid and unmistakable transformation and decline. For those keen to examine those social and economic trends which might provide a key to the events of 1985, the basic data is startling. Indeed, there are few sets of comparative economic and social data which do not illustrate the sharp and seemingly uncontrollable decline of the British economy and of all those social institutions which depend upon economic well-being. Many observers, at home and abroad, not only find this central fact of British decline on a broad front difficult to accept, but it is even more difficult to explain. Commentators thus continually tend to fall back on their own particular theories, using recent events to prove them. Thus we find that the disasters of 1985 were presented as proof of an extraordinary variety of social and political theories. Many observers, though not all, were convinced that the events of 1985 were strong evidence of the nation's decline. How to arrest or reverse it, however, remains an issue of central political and social argument.

When the national game stumbled into the new 1985–6 season it did so in a miasma of political and economic confusion. The game itself had become a political football, punted hither and yon by indeterminate – and often undisciplined – teams of politicians and critics. Inevitably, former spectators stayed away in growing numbers; economic crisis hovered over the game. To make matters worse the mental insularity, which had so often been the game's pre-eminent characteristic in earlier generations, was now compounded by the enforced isolation from the rest of the footballing world. It may be true that many forays abroad had, in the past generation, revealed a brute insularity and an ignorant and assertive zenophobia (in common with many other British visitors abroad), but it is unlikely that this will be modified by enforced isolation from our international neighbours. There are, it is true, glimmers of light in this rather bleak picture. But it is equally true that the game of English football – like so many aspects of the society which spawned it – is in the process of major change, the full ramification of which still cannot be predicted. And all this has been brought into vivid focus by the conduct and misbehaviour of some of its fans. If the game had, for many years, reflected a number of important qualities and strengths of its expansive and self-confident parent society, by the 1980s football was thought to represent much of what ailed domestic life.

Notes and References

1 Whatever Happened to the People's Game?

1. Quoted in James Walvin, *The People's Game. A Social History of English Football* (London, 1975). p. 50.
2. Ibid, p. 68.
3. 'The New Football Mania', *Nineteenth Century*, 1892, XXXII, pp. 622–8.
4. *National Reformer*, 62, No. 3, July 1893, p. 43.
5. G. R. Sims, *The Living London*, 3 vols., 1901, I, pp. 292–6.
6. *The Ethical World*, S. Coit and J. A. Hobson (eds), 22 April 1899, II, no. 16.
7. Ibid, 20 May 1899.
8. Ibid, 21 April 1900, III, no. 16.
9. Quoted in Walvin, *People's Game*, p. 66.
10. Ibid, p. 77.
11. *Socialist Worker*, no. 939, 8 June 1985, pp. 2–3.
12. *New Statesman*, 7 June 1985, p. 8.
13. For one of the instant commentaries on these and other assessments see Paul Johnson, 'Was Caliban a Fascist?', *The Spectator*, 8 June 1985.
14. Frank Keating, *The Guardian*, 30 May 1985.
15. *Social Trends*, 15, 1985 (HMSO) p. 154.
16. 'Football – Our Most Popular Export', *New Society*, 23 October 1980, p. 171.
17. Ibid.
18. James Walvin, *Leisure and Society, 1850–1950* (London, 1978) pp. 149–50.
19. Walvin, *People's Game*, p. 158.
20. *Social Trends*, 15, p. 154.
21. *New Society*, 23 October 1980, p. 171.
22. *Facts in Focus* (London, 1978) p. 178. See also 'Cinemas', in John Hey, *Britain in Context* (Oxford, 1979) p. 178.
23. 'Leisure', in A. H. Halsey (ed.), *Trends in British Society Since 1900* (London, 1972), pp. 540–1.
24. Ibid, p. 543.
25. Tony Mason, *Association Football and English Society, 1863–1915* (Brighton, 1980), p. 228.

2 Victorian Values: Clubs and Managers

1. Steven Wagg, *The Football World. A Contemporary Social History* (Brighton, 1984), ch. VIII.
2. *The Times*, 22 July 1985, p. 2.

3. Brian Dalton, 'The Financial Management of a Professional Football Club', *Accountants Record*, no. 65, April 1985, pp. 3–6.
4. *The Times*, 27 July 1985; Committee of Inquiry into Crowd Safety and Control at Sports Grounds, Interim Report, Cmnd 9585, ch. 7.
5. 'A Funny Game', *New Society*, 19 August 1982.
6. Dalton, 'Financial Management', p. 6.
7. Ibid, p. 5.
8. Stan Hey, 'Leagues Apart', *The Listener*, 25 August 1983.
9. Dalton, 'Financial Management', p. 6.
10. Wagg, *Football World*, ch. 10.
11. Rosemay Burr, 'The Football Bosses', *New Society*, 19 May 1983, p. 283.

3 Feet of Clay: Modern Players

1. Wagg, *Football World*, p. 122.
2. Jeremy Tunstall, *The Media in Britain* (London, 1984 edn.), p. 123.
3. Stan Hey, 'Leagues Apart', p. 2.
4. 'A Funny Game', *New Society*, 19 August 1982.
5. 'Football – Our Most Popular Export', *New Society*, 23 October 1980, p. 171.
6. 'Plastic Football', *New Society*, 25 August 1983, p. 271.
7. 'Football – Our Most Popular Export'.
8. Ibid.
9. Wagg, *Football World*.
10. *New Collins English Dictionary* (London, 1982).
11. Eamon Dunphy, *Only a Game?* (London, 1976); Paul Gardner, *Nice Guys Finish Last* (London, 1974).

4 Fanatics

1. John Hutchinson, *The Football Industry* (Glasgow, 1982), pp. 49–64; Tony Mason, *Association Football*, ch. 5.
2. See the case of Glasgow in Bill Murray, *The Old Firm* (Glasgow, 1985).
3. John Williams, Eric Dunning and Patrick Murphy, *Hooligans Abroad* (London, 1984); Peter Marsh and Anne Campbell (eds), *Aggression and Violence* (London, 1982).
4. Walvin, *People's Game*, ch. 4; F. P. Magoun, Jr, *History of Football from the beginning to 1871* (Cologne, 1938).
5. Tony Mason, *Association Football*, pp. 11–13.
6. These issues are dealt with in Paul Fussell, *The Great War and Modern Memory* (Oxford, 1979).
7. Walvin, *People's Game*, ch. 3.
8. Bill Murray, *Old Firm*.
9. P. J. Waller, *Town, City and Nation, England, 1850–1914* (Oxford, 1983).

10. John K. Walton, *The English Seaside Resort*, Leicester, 1983, pp. 197–8.
11. Tony Mason, *Association Football*, pp. 193–5; P. J. Waller, *Town, City*, pp. 268–9; 313–14.
12. Walvin, *Leisure*, ch. 11.
13. E. G. Dunning, J. A. Maguire and J. M. Williams, 'The Social Roots of Football Hooligan Violence', *Leisure Studies*, 1 (2), p. 2.
14. See Chapter 5.
15. Martyn Harris, 'Leeds, the Lads and the Meeja', *New Society*, 25 November 1982, p. 337.
16. John Williams, 'Football Hooligans', *Youth in Society*, March 1981, no. 52, pp. 8–10.
17. Terrance Morris, 'Deterring the Hooligans', *New Society*, 3 May 1985.
18. For the broader theme of youth culture see John Muncie, *The Trouble with Kids Today. Youth and Crime in post War Britain* (London, 1984).

5 Violence in Context and History

1. J. Muncie, *Trouble with Kids*.
2. John Stevenson, *Popular Disturbances in England, 1700–1870* (London, 1979), p. 301.
3. Ibid, p. 304.
4. Ibid, pp. 306–9.
5. See the essays in John Brewer and John Styles, *An Ungovernable People* (London, 1980).
6. Brian Harrison, *Peaceable Kingdom*, Oxford, 1982.
7. John Hutchinson, *Football Industry*, pp. 56–9.
8. Ibid, p. 70.
9. *Time Magazine*, 10 June 1985, p. 10.
10. Peter Marshall, 'A new British Export – Football Hooliganism', *The Listener*, 5 July 1984, p. 5.
11. Ibid.
12. Eric Dunning *et al.*, 'If You Think You're Hard Enough', *New Society*, 27 July 1981.
13. John Gillis, *Youth and History* (London, 1974); John Gillis, 'The Evolution of Juvenile Delinquency', *Past and Present*, no. 67, 1975.
14. Stephen Humphries, *Hooligans and Rebels* (Oxford, 1981), pp. 16–17.
15. Ibid, pp. 18–19.
16. S. Hall and P. Jefferson, *Resistance through Rituals* (London, 1976).
17. G. Pearson, *Hooligan. A History of Respectable Fears* (London, 1983), pp. 74–7.
18. E. Trivizas, 'Sentencing the Football Hooligan', *British Journal of Criminology*, vol. 21, no. 41, Oct. 1981, pp. 342–9.
19. A. H. Halsey, *Trends*, pp. 541–2; 552–3.
20. J. Muncie, *Trouble with Kids*, pp. 22–25.

6 Racism and Fascism

1. E. Cashmore, *Black Sportsmen* (London, 1982).
2. James Walvin, *Passage to Britain: Immigration in British History and Politics* (London, 1983).
3. Ibid, pp. 189–95.
4. W. J. Baker, *Sports in the Western World* (New Jersey, 1982), pp. 149; 283–4.
5. Ibid, pp. 285–6.
6. Ibid, p. 292.
7. Quoted in E. Cashmore, *Black Sportsmen*, p. 22.
8. John Bale, *The Development of Soccer as a Participant and Spectator Sport: Geographic Aspects* (Sports Council–SSRC, 1979).
9. E. Cashmore, *Black Sportsmen*, ch. 10.
10. Walvin, *Passage*, ch. 9.
11. Ibid, pp. 132–3.
12. Barry Troyne, 'Reporting the National Front', in *Race*, C. Husband (ed.) (London, 1982).
13. Martyne Harris, 'Leeds, the Lads and the Meeja', pp. 337–9.
14. E. Cashmore, *Black Sportsmen*, p. 176.
15. Commission for Racial Equality, *Annual Report* (London, 1985).

7 The Distorting Mirror: The Media and the Game

1. Glasgow Media Group, *Bad News*, 1976; S. Cohen and J. Young (eds), *The Manufacture of News* (London, 1973); Jeremy Tunstall, *The Media in Britain*.
2. Tony Mason, *Association Football*, pp. 187–93.
3. Asa Briggs, *History of Broadcasting* (Oxford, 1979).
4. Jeremy Tunstall, *The Media in Britain*, pp. 123–6.
5. Quoted in G. Murdock, 'Mass Communications and Social Violence', in P. Marsh and A. Campbell (eds), *Aggression and Violence*, p. 63.
6. Jeremy Tunstall, *The Media in Britain*, pp. 122–3.
7. Ibid, p. 150.
8. Barry Gunter, 'Injury Time', *The Listener*, 14 March 1985, p. 15.
9. Jeremy Tunstall, *The Media in Britain*, p. 128.
10. Graham Murdock, 'Mass Communications and Social Violence', p. 68.
11. Ibid, p. 71.
12. Ibid, p. 73.
13. Ibid, p. 75.
14. Ibid, p. 75–76.
15. S. Cohen, *Folk Devils and Moral Panics* (London, 1972); S. Hall *et al.*, *Policing the Crisis* (London, 1978).
16. Robin Fox, 'The Violent Imagination', in P. Marsh and A. Campbell (eds), *Aggression and Violence*, ch. 1.

8 Codes of Discipline

1. *The Spectator*, 23 July 1983.
2. This was a hostile and splenetic piece; 'From Great Port to Piggery', *The Spectator*, 8 June 1985, p. 16.
3. J. Lawrence and D. Steed, 'Predisposed to Violence', *Times Education Supplement*, 7 June 1985, p. 25.
4. Arthur Marwick, *British Society Since 1945* (London, 1982), pp. 235–8.
5. For a vivid though partisan account of this process (in Hackney) see Paul Harrison, *Inside the Inner City* (London, 1982), ch. 11.
6. James Walvin, *A Child's World. A Social History of English Childhood* (London, 1983), ch. 7.
7. For a rather caricatured view of this, see S. Humphries, *Hooligans and Rebels*, ch. 3.
8. Arthur Marwick, *British Society*, p. 241.
9. All quotes from Paul Johnson, 'Was Caliban a Fascist?', p. 18.
10. This was even noticeable in the 1985 Dimbleby Lecture; Mary Warnock, 'Teacher Teach Thyself', *The Listener*, 28 March 1985, pp. 10–14.
11. For details of this argument, see a brilliant book by Bernice Martin, *A Sociology of Contemporary Cultural Change* (Oxford, 1983), chs. 9–10.
12. Ibid, p. 215.
13. John Muncie, *Trouble with Kids*, ch. 5.
14. Ibid, p. 140.
15. Paul Willis, *Learning to Labour* (London, 1977).
16. Huw Benyon, *Working For Ford* (London, 1973); L. Taylor, *Deviancy and Society* (London, 1971); S. Hall and T. Jefferson, *Resistance through Rituals*.
17. E. P. Thompson, 'Time, Work Discipline and Industrial Capitalism', *Past and Present*, no. 38, 1967.
18. J. Muncie, *Trouble with Kids*, p. 142.
19. Ibid, pp. 143–4.

9 Politics and Sport

1. W. J. Baker, *Sports in the Western World*, ch. 2.
2. Ibid, pp. 31–2.
3. Ibid, ch. 4.
4. Quoted in Walvin, *People's Game*, p. 20.
5. E. P. Thompson, 'Time, Work Discipline and Industrial Capitalism'.
6. See essays in J. K. Walton and J. Walvin (eds), *Leisure in Britain* (Manchester, 1983).
7. *The Ethical World*, 22 April 1899, p. 241.
8. Tony Mason, *Association Football*, ch. 2; C. P. Korr, 'West Ham United Football Club and the beginning of Professional Football in East London 1895–1914', *Journal of Contemporary History*, 13, no. 2, April 1978. For Scotland see Bill Murray, *The Old Firm*, ch. 2.

9. For profits, see Bill Murray, *Old Firm*; Tony Mason, *Association Football*, pp. 44–9.
10. For links between politics and football, see Tony Mason, *Association Football*, pp. 226–9.
11. S. Wagg, *Football World*, pp. 13–14.
12. J. Tampke, 'Politics Only?', *Sport in History*, in R. Cashman and McKernan (eds) (St Lucia, Queensland, 1979).
13. Ibid, chs 6–7.
14. See illustration in Walvin, *People's Game*.

Index